BUSINESS FOR SALE BLUEPRINT™

By Fred Herbert

BUSINESS FOR SALE BLUEPRINT

Designing Your Business To Sell For A Premium Price

by

Fred Herbert

Business For Sale Blueprint

ISBN 978-1-943767-27-4

Printed in USA

Dedication

I dedicate this book to my wife Tracy; her love, patience and unwavering support made this book possible.

Forward

Congratulations – by buying and reading this book, you just confirmed you are that rare entrepreneur who values understanding over ego. You are about to embark on a journey that will invigorate your company, its people, and its leadership.

How do I know the outcome of you reading this book? The reason is because I have been where you are sitting many times over the last 30 years. I have created, grown, and sold businesses in a variety of markets and economic cycles. While each enterprise offered different products and services to national and international target markets, one constant dominated them all – at some point, I would exit the business. It would be through one of the following three doors:

Door # 1: I would die

Door # 2: The business would die

Door # 3: The business would be sold (hopefully at a significant profit)

I have to confess that it was not until I exited several businesses that the full implications of this concept hit me. Because of these experiences, I began to understand the critical value of a well defined Owner Transition Plan (Exit Strategy), and it was also when I could have benefited from the information contained in this book!

Back then, most of us did not even know what "best practices" and "exit strategies" looked like or how to implement them. Our loss – your gain.

In this practical, user friendly book, *Business For Sale Blueprint*, Fred Herbert provides you, the business owner, with all of the concepts and tools you will need to boldly walk through door number three into your next entrepreneurial adventure (with money in your pockets). Fred's teaching style has been honed over several decades of building his own companies and helping others discover the practices and mindsets that will make them stand head and shoulders above their competition. I like to call Fred "One of the Good Guys" because he cares deeply about insuring the success of his clients by providing them with proven best practices that build strong, sustainable, and *sellable* companies.

If you are like most of independent business owners – *emphasis on independent*, when business is good (i.e., sales are rising, employees and customers are happy, competitors are fleeing, the economy is growing), we cannot imagine ever leaving.

Managing our company toward a successful sale is kind of like picking out a cemetery plot; we figure that we will get around to it eventually (like when we are dead). Unfortunately, not unlike death and taxes, even the best managed companies are ultimately at the mercy of the marketplace. Managing for high growth or high margins is not the same as managing to maximize our return at sale time. Often, when market conditions develop in a way that would set the stage for cashing out, we are simply caught unprepared and the opportunity evaporates.

Let's face it: *everyone* is a genius when sales, margins and market share are on the rise. Not so much when the situation turns south. By employing the tools, strategies, and management techniques in *Business For Sale Blueprint*, you will be equipped to take advantage of both up *and* down movements in your market.

When I read most business books my approach is the following: "I will just skim over this material and pick out the things I like." When I picked up *Business For Sale Blueprint* for the first time, I read it "cover to cover." Next, I will provide copies to my friends and clients. The reason is simple: these strategies work, but not if you "cherry pick" it and do not fully commit to it.

You may be old enough to remember a time when we actually knew how to work on our own cars. Now, short of having an advanced degree in automobile diagnostics, most of us can not even figure out how to remove that big plastic cover that sits over the engine (at least I think there is an engine under there!). Actually, the fact that the engine cover is there *and* that it takes a special tool to unscrew it is no accident. It is a not so subtle way for the manufacture to remind us that carburetors and manual pumps have given way to electronic fuel injection and computer controlled sensors. In other words, they are telling us to: KEEP OUT – YOU ARE NOT TRAINED FOR THIS!

In the same way, leading a business in a manner that will maximize its value at sale time requires training, operational practices, and strategies that most of us were never taught.

I have sat in the very uncomfortable seat of "the owner who has to sell because the market has fallen apart" without an exit plan. I have also learned from that experience and sought out acknowledged experts like Fred Herbert to prevent an unpleasant replay.

Now as a business broker and strategist, I advise my clients to read *Business For Sale Blueprint*, employ its strategies, and start TODAY.

Remember, there is no door number four, no matter how much magic thinking we may conjure up. If our goal is to build a business that will last, provide for our employees, customers, and vendors while assuring a fruitful equity harvest for our family, we need not walk through door number three alone.

Here, in *Business For Sale Blueprint*, Fred has done the hard work of gathering the "Best of the Best Practices" for us. All we have to do is pay attention and take action.

Here's to your success,

Tony Ford
Tony Ford & Associates
Fort Worth, Texas

Table of Contents

Preface

My name is Fred Herbert and I want to thank you for reading *Business For Sale Blueprint.* I would like to provide you with some of my background information and the reasons I decided to write this book.

Of my 35 years in business, I dedicated 25 years to succeeding as a self-employed entrepreneur. I have a heart for the small business owners because I, like you, have faced every challenge a business owner encounters. The following are some issues you may have encountered or are currently battling: cash flow, employee, supplier, accounting, legal, customer, quality, and sales; these are issues I have had to confront as well. The life of a small business owner is not easy. The sleepless nights, stress, burnout, and times of depression make me wonder why I love being a business owner so much. I guess some of my motivational factors are the feeling of control, calling my own shots, freedom to use my time and skills in a way I can focus on my strengths and passions. The main motivation for me is that I am fully responsible for the success or failure of my business.

I began my business career in the printing industry. By 21 years old, I was the owner of a small quick printing company in Wichita, Kansas, which I sold after 14 years. I was absent from the printing business for several years and tried my hand at several different professions, most of which included sales.

In 1998, I had the opportunity to work for a printing company that changed my whole career direction. This opportunity placed me on a path of the Quality Industry where I developed my expertise in process and performance excellence. I helped this company win a state quality award, and I also helped them achieve the nation's highest business excellence award: the Malcolm Baldrige National Quality Award. I continued with my professional career and became a Baldrige Examiner for several years; a Certified Manager of Quality and Operational Excellence; and I received the Lean/Six Sigma Black Belt Certification (a Six Sigma Black Belt is someone who has proven expertise in Lean/Six Sigma Methodology. Six Sigma was created by Motorola to improve processes and reduce defects).

In early 2007, I decided to become an independent consultant. While I trained companies in Lean and assisted with process improvement, my business evolved toward a focus on helping business owners prepare for the sale or transfer of their business. Many of the same tools used in the quality industry applied to guiding business owners toward success. I felt as if my contribution to my clients and the world would be best served by helping business owners dramatically increase the value of their business. I came to realize that companies could increase their value by hundreds of thousands of dollars and even millions if they focused on the necessary strategies and issues in running a business.

This book emerged primarily because of conversations I had with business brokers and business valuation professionals. Brokers shared with me their frustrations on how few business owners come to them with a business that has all its ducks in a row. A friend of mine told me he thought that out of all the business owners that came to him wanting to sell, about 20% were ready to list and sell, and he thought 20% just would not survive. Therefore, 60% of the businesses he felt could do well if they went back and began working on the issues and strategies that would prepare them to sell their company in the future.

This became my focus. How do I help the 60% of business owners prepare to sell or develop an effective business transition strategy? The next challenge I faced was that not every business feels they can afford a consultant. Though the return on investment (ROI) has proven to be substantial, hiring a consultant is a difficult decision for many business owners.

The next natural progression for me was to discover how I can help a greater audience of business owner at prices they feel they can afford. Because I desired to assist more business owners, the *Business For Sale Blueprint* strategy enabled me to reach this goal. With *Business For Sale Blueprint*, I have created several related products:

- Tele-seminars and Webinars
- Business Assessment tools
- Seminars and workshops
- Audio and video programs

These products are available to assist a national audience.

Of course, I still perform one-on-one consulting and training, and speak to large and small audiences of business owners.

The more you read and apply the tools and strategies in *Business For Sale Blueprint,* the faster you will move your business toward greater value.

Introduction

Welcome to ***Business For Sale Blueprint***.

My goal in writing this book is to:

HELP YOU INCREASE THE VALUE OF YOUR BUSINESS AND IMPROVE YOUR ODDS OF SELLING!

More dollars in your pocket should you sell
More valuable to you should you keep it

This book is designed to enable you to dramatically increase the value of your business and prepare it for a quick and profitable sale by following the Business For Sale Blueprint™ strategy. After you decide to follow and execute many of the guidelines in this book, you will feel much better about your business. You may even decide to keep it because it is running smoothly and profitably. My desire is for you to meet your objectives regardless of the outcome. We will work together through each chapter in order to focus on the key strategies you may execute now and in the near future to obtain the most out of your business.

This book is not as much a "How To" book as it is a "What To Do" book. I will accentuate many different areas you may want to work on as you guide your business toward success, and I will often highlight effective resources. There are some great "How To" books and experts to help you in any area you choose to work on; however, my goal is to help you determine which areas need improvement and encourage you to take action and find the resources necessary.

What motivates you the most? Is it the Carrot or the Stick (we are driven by either pleasure or pain)? Every business owner has their own answer to this question. Following is my Carrot and Stick list of reasons to follow the Business For Sale Blueprint™ guidelines found in this book:

The Carrot

- Business running more smoothly
- Can sell in a few years for double its current value
- Easy to find a buyer at premium price
- Retire with lots of cash in the owners pockets
- Live the dream of their choosing

The Stick

- Business not saleable
- Business value has declined dramatically
- Hard to find buyers at even greatly discounted prices
- Close the doors and liquate
- No return for all the blood, sweat, and tears
- Nothing for the owners retirement

The original title for this book was *Double or Nothing*. Why Double or Nothing?

"Double or nothing" is a gambling term in making a wager. While I am not using the term in this manner, there is a sense that you take a huge gamble with your business if you do not focus on what is necessary for your business to succeed. Following is a description from the title of the program, which outlines the program's objectives.

"In less than three years, your business can Double in value or be worth Nothing, depending on what you do Today"

Double?

It is possible that by working on the necessary strategies (as outlined in this book) you can double the value of your business in the next few years. A business worth $500,000 today can be worth over $1 Million in less than three years. A $2 Million dollar company can be worth $4 Million and so on. It is simple math: increase cash flow and the multiplier (I will discuss later) and you have the formula for a substantial increase in the value of your business.

Below is an example of a company that currently has a "Market Value" of just over $1.6 million dollars. By focusing their efforts on what is called the "Value Drivers," they increase the market value to over $3.3 million dollars in just three years. Notice that this was possible with modest sales growth of only 5% per year.

Doubling Business Value in Three Years

Year	Current	Year 1	Year 2	Year 3
Sales	$ 3,000,000	$ 3,150,000	$ 3,307,500	$ 3,472,875
Sales Increase		5%	5%	5%
EBITDA* %	25%	27%	28%	30%
EBITDA*	$ 750,000	$ 850,500	$ 926,100	$ 1,041,863
Multiplier	2.25	2.5	3	3.25
Business Value	$ 1,687,500	$ 2,126,250	$ 2,778,300	$ 3,386,053
Increased Value	$ -	$ 438,750	$ 1,090,800	$ 1,698,553

EBITDA means Earnings before Interest, Taxes, Depreciation, and Amortization, and is discussed in the Financial Management chapter.

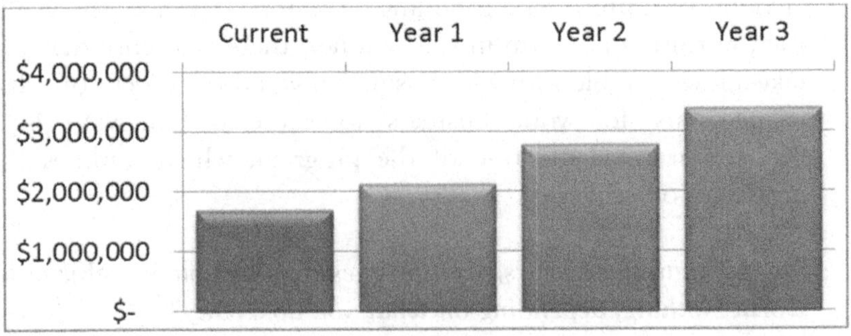

I have had this chart reviewed by several business valuation professionals. One told me that the values were on the conservative side. The ability of a business to double in value within a few years varies widely depending on their size, industry, margins, region, and level of maturity.

Nothing?

The hard reality is that many business owners place their companies on the market without success in finding a potential buyer. This forces them to close the doors, liquidate, or just wait as long as possible with no hope of ever achieving their dreams.

The fact is that many business owners consult with a business broker, business intermediary, or investment banker to list their business for sale and over 80% find no buyers. They either have to keep the business or liquidate. Either way, this scenario was not the business owner's objective, and they did not fulfill the potential that was there a few years earlier.

The following are statistics come from www.bizstats.com based on 2011 Government data:

Number businesses listed	*998,000*
Number businesses sold	*206,500*

The significance of these numbers is as follows:

- of the 998,000 business owners who put their company up for sale only 21% were successful
- a staggering 791,500 business failed in their attempt to sell

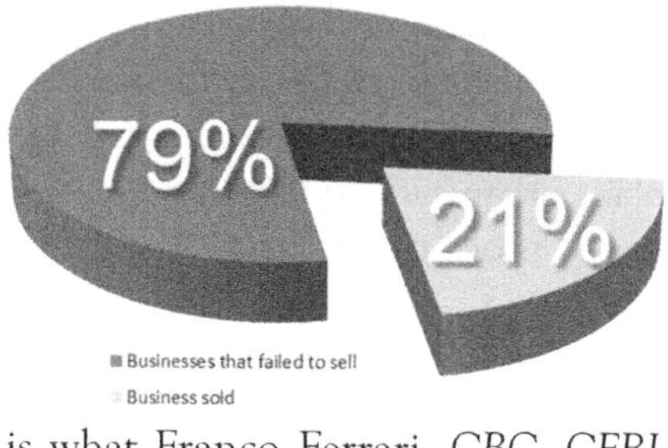

The following is what Franco Ferrari, *CBC, CFBI, CBI*, wrote to me on this subject.

"As per intense research done by Lou Vescio, of the Sunbelt Melbourne, Florida office. The embarrassing % of listed businesses that actually sell is 11%, far below the 20% to 25% that everyone inflates (this of course is for all offices in general and a direct result of overpricing). There are specific offices that adhere to very exact pricing guidelines and their % of success is as high as 75%."

I may add that those offices attribute their high success ratio to their membership in IBBA and insisting that all their agents take the necessary IBBA courses to obtain the CBI and/or the M&AMI designation. IBBA education and professionalism makes a big difference.

Whether it is 11% or 21%, the fact is, many business owners do not achieve their dream of selling their business at all, let alone at a premium price. This is why you have to work on building your business value and at the same time build sale ability.

Do Not Feel Overwhelmed

This book is loaded with material and it is natural for these ideas to appear as an overwhelming task. However, this book is laid out in chapters for each "Value Driver" and steps that you may implement as you have the time and resources to accomplish.

You will end up with a large list of action items, and it is important to prioritize them and focus on the ones that will have the quickest impact on the business. Additionally, it is also a great idea to tackle some items early that have a visual impact (for example, workplace organization) in order for everyone to feel and witness that progress is occurring.

This book is not intended to overwhelm you with all the necessary tasks you need to accomplish; instead, it is meant to help you create a roadmap that will lead you to your destination.

Understanding the Buyer's Perspective

Throughout this book, I will emphasize what the buyer desires to obtain from a business. Most business owners are too close to their business to realistically assess it from someone else's perspective. Try to honestly assess how well you can analyze the following with unbiased eyes:

- ☑ The appearance of your facilities
- ☑ Employee performance and value toward future growth
- ☑ The financial performance of your company
- ☑ The true Fair Market Value of the organization
- ☑ The ability of your management team to run the company without you

If you can truly analyze these items (and the many others I will discuss later) from an outsiders perspective, you are a rare individual. Most of us are too close to our company to assess the business accurately and more so from the point of view of a potential buyer.

I will discuss this item in more detail in a later chapter.

The icon below will be used throughout this book to illustrate how the buyer may assess each area of the business.

Taking Action

You will not obtain the desired results from this book unless you and your team take action on many of the items outlined to increase the value of the business. Throughout this book, I will identify Action Items you should consider adding to your action plans. At the end of each chapter, I will outline valuable action items you should implement.

The icon below will be used throughout this book to point out area where action is required.

Action Plan Template

Tacking action is an important step in a business, which is why I want to provide a helpful tool. Below is an example of the Action Planning template (Word document) available free with this book.

For your copy at:
http://businessforsaleblueprint.com/book-resources

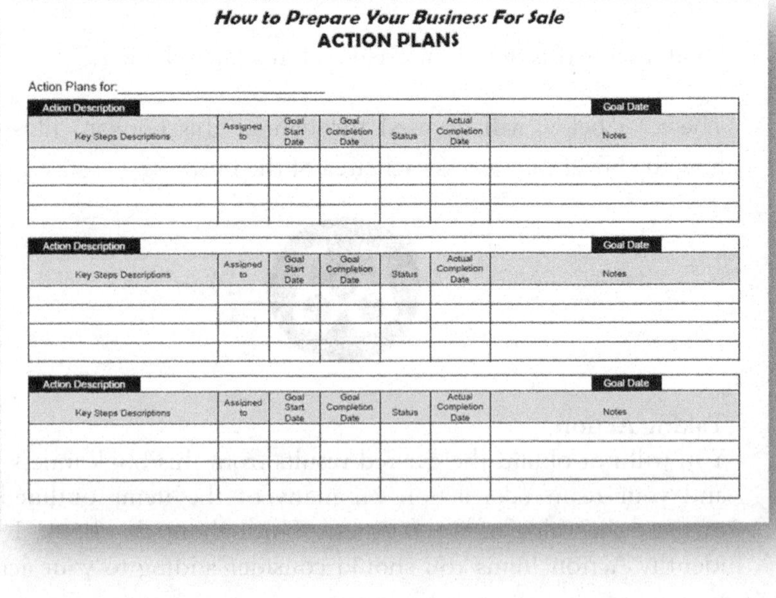

How to Prepare Your Business For Sale
ACTION PLANS

Action Plans for: ____________________

Action Description						Goal Date
Key Steps Descriptions	Assigned to	Goal Start Date	Goal Completion Date	Status	Actual Completion Date	Notes

Action Description						Goal Date
Key Steps Descriptions	Assigned to	Goal Start Date	Goal Completion Date	Status	Actual Completion Date	Notes

Action Description						Goal Date
Key Steps Descriptions	Assigned to	Goal Start Date	Goal Completion Date	Status	Actual Completion Date	Notes

You do not have to use this tool but I recommend you have a tool available to record the action items you plan to implement as a result of this book. Some clients use a tool like Tasks in Outlook or even project management software.

Many owners miss some important pieces of the Action Planning processes; however, below are some of the items I include:

Action Description
It is very important to clearly describe the action you plan to implement. Make it detailed enough that anyone reading it can understand what you plan to accomplish.

Goal Date
You must set a date of when you want to accomplish this action, but do not worry about setting a perfect date. Utilize your gut reaction on when you would like to accomplish this action item. During the review process, you will have the opportunity to reevaluate your resources (time and money) and adjust dates accordingly.

Key Steps Descriptions
Some Action Plans may only take one step, but others may take many steps. I recommend creating a list of each step required and placing assignments, goal dates, and status updates for each item.

Assigned To
Many assignment boxes may just have your name, but on items that you delegate, keep track of them and hold others accountable to meet the agreed upon deadlines.

Goal Start Date
Some Action Items may begin today and others may begin months away. Indicate your best guess as the ideal start dates.

Goal Completion Date
Keep track of each Action Items goal to complete date.

Status

Under "status," I include a one word description of each Action Item, such as "Pending," "On-Hold," "In-Process," or "Completed".

Actual Completion Date

Keep track of actual completion date. You can reassess and rethink these in order to improve your planning in the future by learning how to better predict realistic time-lines.

Notes

It is always a good idea to have a place to keep notes and ideas that need to be documented.

Follow-up

Follow-up is where most people fail. Without a systematic follow-up process, these Action Plans will just sit and provide little additional value. You receive some value by writing them down and thinking through the steps, but the most important action is to ensure you make progress toward accomplishing your goals.

Action Items

- ❑ *Before you continue reading, determine the tool you will use to keep track of all the Action Items that will be discussed throughout this book.*

- ❑ *Have your Action Planning system handy as you go through these upcoming chapters to record the objectives you wish to accomplish.*

Chapter 1
Perspective

As mentioned in the Overview, it is critical to understand the buyer's perspective when preparing your business to sell in the future. While this book is designed to help you understand what the buyer will want to see in your business, I felt this particular area deserves extra attention.

Throughout this book, you will notice the "Buyers Perspective" icon and text shown below.

Buyer's Perspective

It is difficult to assess your business from the buyer's perspective because you may be attached to your business, which may prevent you from maintaining an unbiased perspective.

Have you ever written a letter and reviewed it several times and you were sure it was perfect? Have you then had the experience of receiving a call or email pointing out a glaring error? If you are like me, it has happened many times. I now send important documents to an editor in order for him or her to identify the mistakes I overlooked. It is not because I cannot write; it is so much my creation that I blank out misspelled words, poor sentence structure, or improper tense.

As we may overlook writing errors, we may also miss obvious (to others) problems, errors, and gaps in our business. Realizing that, I am aware that even as this book highlights what the buyer looks for if they are going to pay a premium price, you still may have some difficulty applying these necessary strategies and steps in your business. Below are some ways to obtain additional help in gaining the needed perspective.

Business Assessment

One option is to hire a business consultant to perform a comprehensive Business Assessment. The consultant could even use this book to assist in the review of your company's performance in all the items I outline in this book. Ideally, the consultant should possess extensive business experience and have some experience in assisting business owners prepare for sale. Their primary value is the ability to assess your business in new and different ways than you. An experienced consultant will have seen "world class" business operations from which to compare and possibly could even compare you with competitors.

Cost

A possible downside of this recommendation is cost. A typical experienced consultant will charge anywhere from $1,000 to $3,000 per day (plus travel costs) and could take 2 to 5 days to properly prepare. The cost could be well worth it by speeding up the process and helping you identify what the buyer sees, thus increasing the sale price (assuming necessary actions are taken).

Availability

It may be difficult to find a local consultant who has the skills to aid you in this process. If that is the case, please consider my company *Fred Herbert Consulting Group*; I offer a Business Assessment service that is tailored to match this book. Please visit www.fredherbert.com for more information.

Business Broker

While it may be too early to discuss your business situation with a broker in order to list your business, you may want to consult with one about reassessing your business and offering a few suggestions based on their experience.

The following are recommendations on finding a good broker:

- **Get Referrals:** It is a good practice to get a referral from a trusted source. Ask your accountant, lawyer, peers, and industry association for names of good business brokers.

- **Check IBBA:** The International Business Brokers Association® (IBBA) is a non-profit "trade association of business brokers providing education, conferences, professional designations and networking opportunities." IBBA has over 1300 members and provides a professional certification process.

- **Due Diligence:** Just as a prospective buyer of your company will exercise due diligence so should you. Examine your broker's background, experience, and credentials. Are there any lawsuits or complaints against them? Check the Better Business Bureau. Investigate their references. Have they handled sales of your type of business before?

- **Experience:** Make certain the broker has sufficient experience in selling businesses.

- **Ability to Market:** Your broker must possess the skills to actively market your business. The stats I shared earlier showed some 80% of businesses won't be sold. The better your broker and their agency are at marketing, the better your odds will be.

Find a broker you would likely list your business with when you are ready to sell. I recommend asking them to help you for no fee; many brokers would be happy to help because it is in their best interests in the long run. When your business is marketable at a premium price, they should visualize the commission dollar signs. The broker has to be patient and provide value first before they obtain your listing. If they are not willing to help, consider finding a broker who understands the value this relationship. I have had several brokers tell me that they felt most brokers are very short-term focused and only want to deal with a business they can list now. Take the time to find a broker that has a long-term view and will provide help in preparing your business to sell when the timing is best for you.

Customers and Suppliers

In some industries, suppliers and customers are willing to help their clients improve operations. For example, I had a client have FedEx and UPS evaluate and make recommendations in their warehouse and fulfillment operations, and they made effective and necessary improvement suggestions.

Large companies, such as Lockheed Martin, Boeing, Motorola, Administaff, Toyota, RR Donnelly, and many others, are known to help their customers and suppliers improve in quality and performance. I am aware of several situations where customers have sent in Six Sigma Black Belts to help improve the supply chain. Verify with your larger suppliers and customers to discover if they possess any programs to help you improve operational performance. Any improvements they help you make will enable you to come closer to that premium sale price you desire.

Family and Friends

This piece of advice might be a challenge because of the difficulty in accepting constructive criticism from family or friends. If you can set your ego aside, this can be an effective, no cost idea. You will have to promise to your family and/or friends that you will not hold any ill feeling for any of the suggestions or advice they share.

The following are suggestions you may ask them to perform:

- Ask an employee to take your family and/or friends on a tour of the facility (inside and out) and ask them to record any item or object they notice that is out of place.

- Ask the family and/or friends to come in or call posing as a customer (secret shopper) and discover how they are treated.

- Ask family and/or friends to come in for a day and work alongside your employees (at non-skilled position) or just observe from nearby; you will be shocked by how much they will learn in just a short period of time.

- Share this book with family and/or friends and ask them to evaluate actions you can implement under each category.

Action Items

☑ *Reread the above possible sources to help you obtain an outsiders' perspective and determine which approach you will take. If several, then set order of preference.*

- ☑ *For the quickest and most diversified list of ideas, use all the above suggestions in combination*
- ☑ *List actions you plan to take on your Action List Worksheet (or Action Planning tool you selected) and set the appropriate dates and steps you plan to take*

Chapter 2
Planning

The development of Exit Strategies and specific plans to execute these strategies is essential in the early stages. This process will not only help you as you plan for your future, but it is impressive to share a documented plan with a potential buyer.

Buyer's Perspective

- *While Ownership Transition Planning (Exit Planning) is primarily for the seller, the state of preparedness will affect the buyer.*

- *The Strategic Plan, Business Plan, and Marketing Plan are tools that will impress a buyer and will assist you toward the achievement of your exit goals. Whether you sell or not, they are important tools toward running a successful company*

"The nicest thing about not planning is that failure comes as a complete surprise, rather than being receded by a period of worry and depression."

Sir John Henry James

Ownership Transition Planning

Your business will someday be under new ownership, and the transition of ownership has four possible outcomes:

- Transfer to family
- Transfer to employee(s)
- Transfer to partner (in partnership situations)
- Transfer to third party

In this section, I will provide a brief overview of Ownership Transition Planning. I highly recommend finding a professional to guide you through this, somewhat, complicated process.

Owners Objective

Ownership Transition Planning begins with a clear understanding of what the owner desires to achieve with their business. You must take the time to identify your short and long term objectives. Forget, for a moment, what you think is realistic and answers the following questions related to your ultimate objective:

- When do you want to leave?
- How much income do you need after you leave your company?
- Do you have family members you would like to transfer the business too?
- Is there a desire to help charitable endeavors with the proceeds of your business?
- Are there employees you would like to reward when you sell your business?

- Would you like to have an employee buy your business?

My desire is only to see you meet your transition goals. If your objective is a consideration of transferring your business to family or employee(s) as an option, that is fantastic. Your objectives are what matters in Ownership Transition Planning.

Ownership Transition Planning Definition
I believe Ownership Transiting Planning (sometimes referred to as Exit Planning or Exit Strategies) is a process of determining the ultimate, best strategy to meet the owner's objectives. It is a systematic approach to ferreting out the pros and cons of each strategic option and determining the course of action that ensures the most effective balance of reward verses risk. The final plan must consider the following aspects:

- Family
- Employees
- Investments
- Taxes
- Retirement

Transition Plan Advisory Team
A well developed Ownership Transition Plan requires the combined input of many advisors with different areas of expertise. The following list indicates many of the advisors who, I believe, can provide valuable information:

- Financial Planner
- Business Valuation Specialist
- Investment Advisor

- Insurance Advisor
- Business Attorney
- Estate Plan and Tax Attorney
- CPA
- Business Broker
- Investment Banker
- Business Consultant
- Banker

No one profession has all the answers needed to create the best possible Ownership Transition Plan; therefore, a process that brings these disciplines together for the benefit of the owner is essential. The problem is that these professions are sometimes adversarial toward each other and offer opposing recommendations. While it may be rare, there are cases of some professionals who suggest strategies that are more in the interests of the advisors than of the business owner.

Ownership Transition Planning Intermediary

If possible, it is advantageous to find an expert in Ownership Transition Planning to guide the process and coordinate the efforts and inputs of the entire Advisory Team. I prefer to use someone who is as neutral and independent as possible, and most importantly, someone who does not offer recommendations in hopes of gaining substantial commissions. There are many examples of cases where the advisor made recommendations that were clearly not in the owner's best interest; the only conclusion one can draw is that their advice was tainted by the profit motive.

There are people who offer this service for free, but they typically expect compensation for their time, efforts, and expertise through commissions on the products they sell.

An independent Transition Planning Advisor is usually fee based because their compensation is not tied to the products you purchase. Fees for this type of service can range from $5,000 to $30,000, which, ultimately, depends on the complexity of your situation. While this is anecdotal, the belief is that most owners save six to ten times what they spend on expert Ownership Transition Planning advice. This is accomplished mostly in tax savings and strategies to build and protect business value.

The other role of your Ownership Transition Planning Intermediary is a project manager. They should develop action plans for each professional advisor on your team and make sure the plans are executed in the agreed upon timeframes. An Ownership Transition Plan on the shelf is of no real value; the value comes when plans are executed.

Please contact me if you would like assistance in finding a qualified intermediary.

Transfer to Family

Transferring a business to a family member is the desire of many business owners. There are two main reasons that, while desired, the idea is usually discarded:

1. The family member does not have money
2. The family member does not have the necessary skills to run the company

The advantages of transferring your business to family member(s) are:

- You have a ready buyer

- The goal of keeping your business in the family is met
- With the right strategy, you can obtain more money for the business

Trying to turnover a business to a family member without the necessary strategy to address the money and skills issues is a recipe for disaster. Therefore, a good Owner Transition Planning Advisor/Intermediary can assist you with these issues. There are some viable ways to structure a plan that mitigates the risks and meets the owner's objectives. Since you are reading this book, you may be set on a third party sale, but you may not realize there are other available strategies. If transferring your business to a family member(s) is your real desire, you should hire an Owner Transition Planning Advisor/ Intermediary to guide you.

Transfer to Employees

The transfer of a business to employees is an almost identical situation as the transfer to family discussed above. Lack of money and questionable skills often rule this option out as well. However, as discussed above, there a strategies to address both issues. The money can be found and the skills can be developed. I discuss leadership team and employee development in later chapters.

The advantages of transferring your business to employee(s) are:

- You have a ready buyer
- Employee morale and the incentive to excel is high
- With the right strategy, you can obtain more for the business

A transfer to employees will also require an Owner Transition Planning Advisor/Intermediary to assist you in planning and executing this strategy.

Transfer to Partner

I have some experience on transferring a business to a partner. I sold my printing business to a partner in 1992. Let me share some hard earned advice, if this is your situation.

- Obtain a Certified Business Valuation – I let our CPA estimate the value of my business, and I know now that he greatly undervalued it. Discover exactly what your business is worth before you negotiate with a partner.

- Have separate attorneys – I tried to save money by taking the advice of our corporate attorney to draft the agreement. If I had my own attorney review the document, he would have never let me sign such a far reaching, non-compete agreement.

- Remove emotional attachments (if possible) – After 14 years, I had hit burnout and was tired of the partnership difficulties. I took an offer just to get out of the situation, and now, I look back and realize I needed a good advisor to help me analyze the numbers and take the emotions out of the process.

There you have it. A wise person learns from the mistakes of others. If you want to sell to a partner, obtain good counsel!

Transfer to third party

The rest of this book is based on how to increase the value of your business and the likelihood of selling to a third party. You will find that taking the recommended actions will enable your business to become: fun to run, less stressful, and more profitable. You may even just decide to stay, and if this is the case, you will now possess more options related to the success of your business!

Worst Case Scenario Planning

Another element that needs to be addressed in Owner Transition Planning is being prepared for the unthinkable. Do you have a plan in place that addresses what would happen with the company if you die or become disabled? The odds of a disability are much high than death. What would happen to your business if you were out for six months? Situations, such as heart attacks, strokes, and accidents cause this scenario more often than you realize. Other issues like divorce should also be addressed. You must have a plan in place that ensures the following:

- The company will accomplish your desires, even if you do not survive the transition
- The business will survive no matter what happens
- Your family will receive the full value of your company, in cash

Tools that are often used in this situation are the following:

- Buy sell agreements
- Life insurance
- Disability insurance
- Written instructions
- Employee stay bonus

I once met a woman whose husband passed away from a tragic heart attack six months earlier. She did not have business experience and tried to discover what to do with the business her husband left her. She was about to sell half of the ownership to someone for liquidation value. When that deal fell apart, she scrambled to salvage some value from the company her husband left her. This was not a pretty picture and a poster case for the importance of planning for circumstances we do not want to think about. I am sure her husband would have developed a plan that ensured the safety of his business and well-being of his family, if he had only known the future. Since most of us do not have that gift, planning for the worst case scenario is our best strategy. Obtain help from a qualified advisor and make the necessary arrangements to protect your family, business and estate.

Building Business Value

Building business value is the focus of the rest of this book. If you have determined that you will not sell or transfer your business immediately, then your strategy is clear; follow the recommendations in *Business For Sale Blueprint.*

If there is a huge gap between what the current business value is and what it must be to meet your goals, then again, your best game plan is obvious; follow the recommendations in *Business For Sale Blueprint.*

You will find that many of my recommendations are not quick fixes. Some things can be done quickly while others take time. You have to encourage the involvement of employees and advisors and ensure progress over time. You can accomplish a lot in three to six months but some items could take several years. If you will wait a few years to sell or transfer your business, why not spend this time building value? That is exactly what I plan to help you do. Let's set a goal together to ensure that your company is worth twice as much as it is today in less than three years. Some companies and industries will find this harder to accomplish than others, but it is a worthwhile goal.

I have selected three years because it is a reachable number for most businesses. Some might take two and others could take four, but let's set high goals and make plans to double the value of your business during the next few years. Doubling the value of your company in three years is asking for 26% value increase compounded each year. If you tackle a reasonable number of the suggestions in *Business For Sale Blueprint*, this goal is very reachable.

Financial Planning

The discipline of Financial Planning is helpful in this process.

We need to determine the following:

- What are my current, non-business assets and resources?
- How much is my business worth?
- How much money will I need to retire (or start another business)?
- How does this all factor into the sell or transfer of my business?

It is necessary to ask a qualified Financial Planning Advisor to assist you in analyzing these scenarios and provide recommendations.

Tax and Estate Planning

An important part of Owner Transition Planning is analyzing the impact of taxes and the value of the entire estate. The goal is to preserve your wealth and minimize taxes as much as possible. Tax planning becomes challenging because the business is likely to form a large part of the estate value.

Only 20% In Liquid Assests

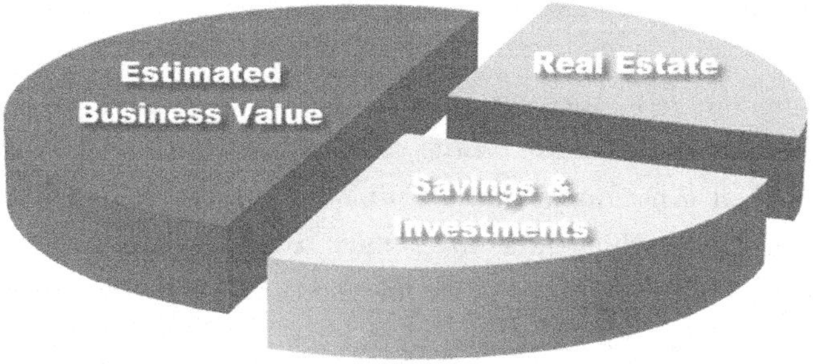

80% In Illiquid Assests

As you can see from the pie chart above, most business owners possess 20% or less in liquid assets, and their illiquid assets of business and property compose the other 80%. With the business being such a large part of your estate, planning that analyzes the whole is essential. What do you have is you are one of the 79% that can't find a buyer, how would this change the picture for you?

What about taxes? It is no secret that the IRS wants to collect taxes while you are alive and when you die. Minimizing the chunk they will take from your estate warrants careful planning. The following is a quote from Monty Walker, who is a tax expert in Ownership Transition Planning:

"Estate planning is not just about money or taxes, but I think we all recognize that the IRS plays a large role in that process. During your lifetime you pay a substantial amount of income taxes; that's a fair price to pay for living in our society. But, there may be a lot more taxes to pay at death. Uncle Sam wants your money and you may be surprised at how much he will get. However, much of that depends upon the steps that you take because proper planning and utilization of established techniques can reduce income, estate and gift taxes.

Perhaps the best starting point in estate planning for business owners is to get a handle on the value of your business because that can have a large impact on the amount of your estate taxes. You have to know what those taxes may be before you can really do much planning to reduce or avoid them. We will talk about some estate tax reduction techniques in this seminar as we go along."

Tax and Estate planning is a complicated process and you must have expert advisors help you navigate the difficult tax laws in order to create the ideal strategy. Please contact me if you need assistance in locating an expert advisor.

In summary, Ownership Transition Planning is of vital importance. The following are key objectives that must be considered:

- Know what you desire
- Know the value of what you already have
- Determine what you need
- Organize a team of experts to guide you

Strategic Planning

"Strategic planning does not deal with future decisions. It deals with the futurity of present decisions. What we have to do today is to be ready for an uncertain tomorrow." Peter Drucker

"What business strategy is all about; what distinguishes it from all other kinds of business planning - is, in a word, competitive advantage. Without competitors there would be no need for strategy, for the sole purpose of strategic planning is to enable the company to gain, as effectively as possible, a sustainable edge over its competitors" Keniche Ohnae

"I get up every morning determined to both change the world and have one hell of a good time. Sometimes this makes planning my day difficult." E. B. White

"In preparing for battle I have always found that plans are useless, but planning is indispensable." Dwight D. Eisenhower

Definition of Strategic Planning
Strategic planning is an organization's process of defining its strategy, or direction, and making decisions on allocating its resources to pursue this strategy, including its capital and people.

Fred Herbert Consulting Group Strategic Planning Process

- Step 1 – Planning
- Step 2 – Evaluate, Review & Assign
- Step 3 – Vision, Mission, & Values
- Step 4 – Environmental Scan
- Step 5 – SWOT Analysis
- Step 6 – Organizational Strategies (Goals)
- Step 7 – Develop Short and Long Term plans
- Step 8 – Create Balanced scorecard
- Step 9 – Communicate Strategic Plan to all employees
- Step 10 – Review

The above process is used in various forms by many Malcolm Baldrige National Award Winning organizations. Even small companies should implement a version of each of these steps and design a formal, written Strategic Plan.

Environmental Scan

An environmental scan is the acquisition and use of information about events, trends, and relationships in an organization's external environment. The knowledge of which would assist management in planning the organization's future course of action.

The environmental scanning involves the following analysis:

- Government
- Legal
- Technology
- Ecology
- Socio-cultural
- Suppliers
- Labor supply
- Service providers
- Stakeholders

Environmental scanning is the process of gathering, analyzing, and dispensing information for tactical or strategic purposes. The environmental scanning process entails obtaining both factual and subjective information on the business environment in which a company is operating or considering entering.

SWOT Analysis

- **Strengths:** attributes of the organization helpful to the achievement of objectives.
- **Weaknesses:** attributes of the organization harmful to the achievement of objectives.

- **Opportunities:** external conditions beneficial toward the achievement of objectives.
- **Threats:** external conditions which could cause damage to the business's performance.

The SWOT analysis provides information that is beneficial in matching the firm's resources and capabilities to the competitive environment in which it operates. As such, it is instrumental in strategy formulation and selection.

Vision, Mission, and Values

- **Vision:** Defines the desired or intended future state of a specific organization or enterprise in terms of its fundamental objective and/or strategic direction.
- **Mission:** Defines the fundamental purpose of an organization or an enterprise, a description of the reasons for its existence.
- **Values:** Beliefs that are shared among the stakeholders of an organization; values drive an organization's culture and priorities.

Strategic Objectives

Strategic Objectives are targets your business must achieve to enable its strategy to succeed. According to the management guru Peter Drucker, Strategic Objectives fall into eight major classifications:

- **Market standing:** desired share of the present and new markets
- **Innovation:** development of new goods and services, and of skills and methods required to supply them
- **Human resources:** selection and development of employees
- **Financial resources:** identification of the sources of capital and their use
- **Physical resources:** equipment and facilities and their use
- **Productivity:** efficient use of the resources relative to the output

- **Social responsibility:** awareness and responsiveness to the effects on the wider community of the stakeholders
- **Profit requirements:** achievement of measurable financial well being and growth

Business Strategy

Business Strategies are your long-term approach toward the implementation of a firm's business plans to achieve its business objectives.

Business Goals

Your leadership team should establish measurable goals that link to each of your strategic Objectives. In Google, search "Balanced Scorecard" and learn how to insure goals cover the important areas of your business.

Action Plans

I discussed the importance of Action Plans in the overview. The process I recommended was to create Action Plans that are assigned to your leadership team, which link to accomplishment of your goals and strategies.

Systematic Review

This is a critical piece of the Strategic Planning Process. You must create a system to review goal accomplishment and Action Plans. I recommend a minimum of quarterly but many companies have a leadership team review monthly.

QUESTION TO BE ANSWERED	STRATEGIC PLAN ELEMENT
Where have we been?	History
Where are we now?	Context
Where should we go and why?	Vision
What is our work toward the vision? Who are we? What is our niche now to work toward the vision?	Mission

What will guide the work we choose to do and the way we do the work (e.g. inclusively, multi-disciplinarily?)	Values
What is in our way of realizing our vision?	Critical Obstacles
What will we do to reach our vision?	Strategic, Long-term Goals/Directions
What will we do in year 1, year 2…	Short-term Goals or Objectives
How will we know if we are successful?	Indicators of Success/Benchmarks
What infrastructure is needed to carry out the work in this plan?	Infrastructure Assessment
What will we do in the next 3 months, six months, year, year 2, year 3	Implementation Plan
How will the plan be disseminated and to whom?	Dissemination Plan Implementation Plan
How will we monitor the plan and assess our progress?	Monitoring and Revising Strategic Plan

The above list was developed for the California State University Chancellor's Office of Community Service Learning by Kathleen Rice, Ph.D.

Business Plan

There are a plethora of practical sources used toward the design of your business plan. I recommend that you purchase a good book or software for help on this subject. It is highly impressive when you present a business plan to a prospective buyer.

Marketing Plan

The same strategy applies toward the development of a Marketing Plan. Most business owners know you should have one but high percentage do not. There are great resources available to help you develop a Marketing Plan.

For additional resources for all the planning described here, please go to: http://businessforsaleblueprint.com/book-resources

Action Items

- ❑ *Formulate an Ownership Transition Plan that helps you meet your objectives*
- ❑ *Find an Ownership Transition Planning Professional to assist you with the development of the best strategies with the least risk*
- ❑ *Organize a Leadership Team to help you develop your strategic plan. The members of the team should be employees who are critical to the success of the company. In general, I recommend anyone who has employees reporting to them or lead a department or key process*
- ❑ *Contact PE^3, if you would like the Strategic Planning Process or any other resources*
- ❑ *Consider hiring a third party expert in Strategic Planning; an outsider can provide great value and improve the process*
- ❑ *List actions you plan to take on your Action List Worksheet (or Action Planning tool you selected) and set the appropriate dates and steps you plan to take*

Chapter 3
Financial Management

In this chapter, I will discuss several areas of financial management that greatly impact the sale of your business.

Buyer's Perspective

The key word for this chapter is TRUST. Questions they will be asking include:

- *Can I truly trust the numbers?*
- *Am I confident that the financial records are accurate?*
- *Can I truly forecast future profits with the numbers we have been given?*
- *If I cannot trust the numbers, can I trust anything the seller is telling us about the company?*

It is critical that we provide accurate and unquestionable information to the potential buyer.

Cash Flow Management

Value of Cash

You have heard the expression "Cash is King," and that is true in both running and selling a business. The expression should read "Cash-Flow is King" because it is a major determiner of business value. To obtain a premium for your business, you must demonstrate the following:

The ability to consistently generate cash from operations

Many years ago when my printing business was growing leaps and bounds, I was shocked when I found I did not have enough cash flow to sustain the growth. The CPA explained that while it appeared profitable on a Profit and Loss Statement, the Cash Flow Statement was another matter. This is when I became a believer in monitoring Cash Flow Projections frequently.

Cash Flow Projections provide you with the visibility needed to avoid problems and create the financial success you intended; it is impossible to run a successful business without accurate projections.

Creating Cash Flow Projections does not have to be a difficult process; there are a great number of free tools available to help you create your own projections.

The Importance of Cash Flow

There are always buyers looking to acquire "good" companies. Buyers are seeking companies that are strong in all the areas discussed in this book. Having strong cash flow is critical to getting a high multiple of that cash.

The Definition of Cash Flow

What is "cash flow?" If a broker or investment banker says they can get you five or six times multiple of your cash flow as a purchase price for your business, you must be certain you are using the same definition. There are several definitions or measures of cash flow, each can be significantly different.

Common measures of cash flow include:

EBIT: Earnings Before Interest and Taxes

EBITDA: Earnings Before Interest, Taxes, Depreciation and Amortization

True Cash Flow: The amount of pre-tax money distributed to owners via salary, bonus, and distributions from the company such as S-distributions, and rental payments in excess of fair market rental value of the equipment or building used in the business.

These measures of cash flow can produce different cash flow numbers. Recasted financials (see Clean Financials section) may provide additional cash flow and should also be taken into consideration.

Action Items

- ❑ *Ask your CPA or Accountant to help you set up a process to track Cash Flow on at least a monthly basis*

- ❑ *Set a specific day each month (or week in tight cash flow periods) to review your projections*

- ❑ *Google "Sample Cash Flow Projections" and you will receive hundreds of examples and even free Excel spreadsheets to help you. Note: If you design your own spreadsheets, make sure you ask your CPA to review them.*

Business Valuation

In my business of helping owners prepare their company to sell for a premium, a valuation done by a business valuation professional can be an important tool.

Reasons why you should have an independent business valuation

Know your starting point

I have talked with many business valuation experts and they all told me that it is rare (almost never) for a business owner to be even close to knowing the true "Market Value" of their business. Brian Wendler with NBVS, tells of a recent case where a client and his CPA thought the business was worth about $18 million. NBVS returned with a value of $30 million and this is the price it sold for. More often than not though, it goes the opposite direction and the owner thinks it is worth much more than the market will bear.

Know the true value of your business

All of your financial and estate planning will hinge on knowing the true value of your business.

It helps in timing the sale

When thinking about your exit, the first two questions you must ask and answer are:

- "How much will I need from the sale of my company to maintain the lifestyle I want for me (and for my family) in retirement?"
- "Is my business worth enough (on an after-tax basis) to support those needs?"

Knowing the answer to these questions will help you determine if the sale could meet your needs now or if you must build up the value to sell at a future date.

"Rules of Thumbs:" Do not work for valuing a business

It surprises many owners to learn that business value is relative, not fixed. It can vary, in part, based on transfer of ownership and on the conditions under which a transfer is made. For example, an appropriate business value for a third party sale may be significantly higher than that established for a transfer of the same business to key employees over time or a gift of the business to children. Business valuation experts understand but "rules of thumb" do not.

Provide incentives to employees who will help you achieve success in your business

A possible strategy might be to ask key employees to become involved in helping you achieve the goals needed to sell the business at the desired price. Incentive programs that both motivate and "handcuff" employees to a company are based on formulas. The most successful of these incentive programs (whether cash- or stock-based) use formulas that include a link between the size of a bonus to growth in business value. Those employees who participate will become most interested to know how you established an accurate business value and whether that value is fair to them. Using an outside appraiser is often the best way to dispel these concerns.

Obtain a Certified Valuation

It is important that you use someone with the experience and credentials to perform an accurate business valuation. Your CPA may tell you that they can do it for you because they have read the valuation formulas in a book or journal somewhere. Do not do it. Make them show you their credentials on business valuations. A business valuation professional will assess hundreds of businesses a year and have access to all the data necessary in order to provide you with an accurate appraisal.

There are many accreditations, but the following are the most recognized:

- **Accredited Senior Appraiser** (ASA) - through the American Society of Appraisers
- **Accredited in Business Valuation** (ABV) - through the American Institute of Certified Public Accounts
- **Certified Business Appraiser** (CBA) - through the Institute of Business Appraisers
- **Certified Valuation Analyst** (CVA) - through the National Association of Certified Valuation

Many Valuation Professionals will offer one of the following three options:

- Summary Appraisal
- Limited Appraisal
- Certified Appraisal

The primary cost difference between the three is primarily due to the time difference in report writing. Certified Appraisals are the most costly and lengthy. For the purposes I describe in this book, a Summary Appraisal will be fine.

Business Valuation Approaches

Below are three fundamental ways to measure what a business is worth:

- **Asset approach**
- **Market approach**
- **Income approach**

For the purpose of preparing the business to sell to a third party, the Market Value approach is what you should be most interested in. You want to know what the business is likely to be worth in today's market. This is called that "Fair Market Value."

Fair Market Value Definition

Fair Market Value is the business price that a willing buyer will pay and a willing seller will accept for the business. Both parties are assumed to act in full knowledge of all the relevant facts, and neither being under compulsion to conclude the sale.

Market approach

The market approach, as the name implies, relies on signs from the real market place to determine what a business is worth. In this case, the so-called economic principle of competition applies.

Someone looking to buy a business will first decide what type of business they are interested in and then explore other options to determine what the "going rate" is for businesses of this type. Business valuation professionals have access to databases of past sales transactions that are similar to your business in your area. This helps them establish the "Market Value"

The market approach to valuing a business is a great way to determine its Fair Market Value.

Strategic Buyer Value

Another item to take into consideration is the value to a strategic buyer. This might be someone in your industry or a compatible industry that would value your business for reasons other than cash flow. A business broker will definitely look for strategic buyer possibilities.

Action Items

☑ *Consider having your business valued soon by a certified business valuation professional*

☑ *Ask your valuation professional what items brought down your value and what you can do to increase your multiplier*

Clean Financials

It is critical that you have clean financials to provide a prospective buyer as evidence. Below is my definition of "Clean Financials."

- Prepared by a respected CPA firm
- Clear separation of discretionary owner benefits (owner perks)
- Statements that follow GAAP (Generally Accepted Accounting Principles)

All your receipts in a box will not be enough. As I discussed in the "Buyer's Perspective," it is an issue of helping the buyer trust the numbers. You need to confirm that you provide potential Buyer's no reason to question the accuracy of your financial statements and future projections.

Recast Financials

One of the tools you will likely employ as you prepare to demonstrate your books to a potential buyer is a Recast Financial Statement. As business owners, we are always thinking about how to minimize taxes as much as possible

Recast Financial Statements are statements of the business that have been adjusted to reflect the actual financial benefits of business ownership. It is often necessary to make adjustments to the reported financial statements in order to express the actual cash flow benefits available for the potential buyer. Another advantage of adjusting the business financial statements is to assists in comparing your business to industry standard ratios.

Below are Balance Sheet items that may require adjustment:

- Accounts receivable. Review an accounts receivable aging report and remove uncollectible accounts, taking them as an ineffective debt expense.

- Inventory that is not high-quality and sellable; inventory that has become damaged or obsolete should be removed.

- Prepaid expenses should be removed if they do not remain with the buyer after the business purchase.

- Cash and cash equivalents are typically retained by the seller; adjust the balance sheet to have the amount of cash required for running the business.

- Remove any amounts due from shareholders as assets or due shareholders as liabilities.

- Book value of assets. If you plan on an asset purchase, you may wish to adjust or "step up" these to their fair market value. This will provide you with tax advantages due to a higher basis for asset depreciation.

- Real estate owned by the business needs to be removed if it is not part of the business purchase.

- Carefully review intangible assets, such as business goodwill to determine if they should be adjusted.

- Accounts payable. Determine if some liabilities have been accumulated without being paid; if so, they must be added to the balance sheet.

Some items on the Profit and Loss Statement that may require adjustment are:

- Adjust cost of goods to historic averages; it is possible that the business has been using lower cost inventory that may not continue in the future.

- Adjust owner's salary and perks to an industry rate for a likely replacement.

- Review and adjust salaries of family members to market rates (if they work in the business).

- Review and adjust depreciation expense consistent with the expected useful life of the underlying assets.

- Adjust the business rent to a fair market rate (If the business owns its real estate premises, include a fair market rent as a business expense).

- Adjust expenses that are incurred at owner's discretion. Examples include travel and entertainment, vehicles, memberships, bonus payouts, and others.

- Factor out any one-time expenses unlikely to occur in the future.

You should consult with your CPA or business appraiser when recasting the financial statements.

Carefully document all adjustments and explain the rational for each

Remember the "Trust Factor." If you include questionable items into the Recast Financials, you could lose credibility that you will never recover.

Limit Owner Perks

Between now and the day you sell your business, consider cutting back on your discretionary owner benefits and perks. I had a client who spent over $300,000 in non-essential expenses (trips and toys) and it was difficult to create a Recast Financial Statement. Potential buyers will have problems trusting your numbers when it appears you tried to cheat the IRS.

Saving $.25 could cost you $4.00

Saving a quarter (on every dollar you expense) on your taxes (assuming a 25% bracket) could easily cost you $4.00 in the sale price (assuming a four times multiplier). If you have a couple of years before you sell your business, take the tax hit on some non-essential items and receive much more back when you sell. Remember the sell price will be based largely on cash flow generated from the business. If you keep your perks down, you will increase cash and eliminate a dependence on a Recast to explain the lack of cash.

Tips from a CPA

I asked my friend Bob Hampton, with Impart Financial, to share his advice to business owners on how to assess and organize their financials. You will notice that he has reiterated some of what I have already shared with you. The following are Hampton's suggestions:

- *"Have an accounting system that will yield reliable financials. Obviously, this allows you to manage your business better, plus anyone coming in for due diligence will have a much better feeling when they have numbers that hang together.*

- *Get the personal stuff out of the company. Ignoring the IRS issues that come with something like that, it does not give a prospective buyer a warm feeling that they are buying a real business that has been professionally operated.*

- *Report all the income on your tax return. When a prospective buyer is told that the business makes a lot more money than is reported on the tax return, if they do not run away, they will discount that representation by at least 100%. Again, a buyer is relying on the honesty of the seller. If they are fessing up to unethical behavior, what other things are they not confessing to?*

- *Plan ahead. Cleaning up the financials is not really a one year affair. The sooner you do it the better. It looks good to a buyer to have several years of financials that tell the same story."*

Tips from Business Brokers

I asked several Business Brokers and Business Intermediaries what they felt could best help a business owner in the preparation to sell their business. Every single response included having clean financials.

The following are suggestions I received:

Sandi Geller who is a partner with Geller & Lehmann in the Boston Area wrote:

> *"I would add the need to get the financial audit and books in order so that they are spotless, transparent and accurate. They should be kept in a 'ready to sell' state at all times."*

Nathan Chitty who is the Managing Director at Central Capital Group in Orlando wrote:

> *"Have audited or reviewed financial statements."*

Effective Financial Controls

Financial controls are not only a critical element of business management, but they also safeguard a company's assets. Most importantly, however, effective financial controls support a claim that a company is consistently profitable. The best way to document that the company has effective financial control and that its historical financial statements are correct is through a certified audit or perhaps a verified financial statement by an established CPA firm.

You can be confident that the buyer will conduct a detailed examination of your company's finances, which is known as financial due diligence. We must ensure that the buyer and the buyer's auditors are comfortable when reviewing your company's past financial performance. A buyer will probably walk away from the deal (or, at best, give a lowball offer) if he or she suspects any inconsistencies.

A certified audit is important because lack of financial integrity has been observed as one of the most common hurdles encountered during the exit process. An audit demonstrates to potential Buyer's that the historical information can be relied upon when making judgments about buying the company based on historical cash flows. It is important to ask your CPA to review your current financial statements and practices so that any financial irregularities or inadequacies are immediately exposed and corrected.

Financial Ratios

It is important for a business owner to know the numbers; financial ratios are not just for your banker. As an owner you should have a good understanding of your company's ratios and how they compare with others in your industry. By monitoring your financial ratios on a regular basis, you will gain insight into how effectively you manage your business.

There are many resources to help you understand the important financial ratios that are important to your business. Below is a quick overview of the Financial Ratios you should be looking at:

Liquidity

Liquidity ratios measure your company's capacity to pay its debts as they come due.

- Current Ratio
- Quick Ratio

Safety

Indicator of the businesses' vulnerability to risk. These ratios are often used by creditors to determine the ability of the business to repay loans.

- Debt to Equity
- Debt coverage ratio

Profitability

The ratios in this section measure the ability of the business to make a profit.

- Sales Growth
- COGS (Cost of Goods Sold) to Sales
- Gross Profit Margin
- SG&A (Selling, General and Administrative) to Sales
- Net Profit Margin
- Return on Equity
- Return on Assets

Efficiency

Efficiency ratios are also called Asset Management ratios. Indicators of how efficiently the company manages its assets.

- Days in Receivables
- Accounts Receivable Turnover
- Days in Inventory
- Inventory Turnover
- Sales to Total Assets

- Days in Accounts Payable
- Accounts Payable Turnover

There are many more business ratios you can track. Get with your CPA or banker and they will help you determine the key financial numbers you should be watching.

Action Items

- ❑ *Ask your CPA to review and audit your books, if necessary*
- ❑ *Begin immediately keeping clear records of owner perks*
- ❑ *Prepare Recast Financial Statements you can provide to your business valuation professional, broker, and potential buyer*
- ❑ *Create a list of "Owner Perks" items that you can eliminate between now and the sale of your business. (If not eliminated, clearly document them)*
- ❑ *If you earn a salary, consider bringing it (up or down) to a level consistent with what it would take to hire someone to replace you*
- ❑ *Perform an analysis of your business ratios and compare them with other businesses in your industry*
- ❑ *List actions you plan to take on your Action List Worksheet (or Action Planning tool you selected) and set the appropriate dates and steps you plan to take*

Chapter 4
Management Team

This chapter is designed to help you develop and retain a management team that will enhance your ability to sell your business at a premium price. If your prospective buyer is not only "Buying a Job," you will need a strong management/leadership team in place or at least one individual who can easily run the business when you are gone.

Buyer's Perspective

The buyer wants to know they are not buying a business that will tie them to day-to-day operations. Even though the final agreement may include the seller who provides several years of consulting, it is critical to have a trusted employee who remains in order to run important business operations. The buyer may be concerned about the following items:

- *Will the seller be available when they are needed?*
- *Will key employees leave immediately after I purchase the business?*
- *Could key employees hold out for more money to stay?*
- *Am I inheriting poor performing employees?*

Without a strong management team in place, it may be difficult to sell your business at all, certainly not likely at a premium price

Leadership Team

Who are your key leaders?

Every organization has some key employees who take the lead in many areas of the operations. You want to demonstrate to a prospective buyer that they are inheriting an exceptional team of employees and leaders. In fact, that is really one of the two main items you sell. To generate the cash flow projected, it will require a continuous effort from your team in order to serve the same (and growing) customer base. The buyer could go across the street and implement all the same equipment and services, but they would not have your employees or customers.

- Who are your key employees a buyer must keep to maintain current operations, service, and quality?
- Which employees have some sort of stay bonus?
- Which employees may consider leaving when you leave?
- Do your employees have any type of performance incentive to help you prepare the business to sell at the highest possible price?

Action Items

- ❑ *Answer the questions above and identify your key leaders*
- ❑ *If you have any concern about keeping these key employees, begin to develop a retention plan (discussed below)*

- ❑ *List actions you plan to take on your Action List Worksheet (or Action Planning tool you selected) and set the appropriate dates and steps you plan to take*

Shifting Core Responsibilities

Begin delegating operational duties and focus on CEO responsibilities

Many business owners wear multiple hats and find it difficult to shift core duties to their management team, which is crucial that you begin this process early in the preparation process. You may find that some key employees do not have the leadership skills required to handle the increased responsibilities and you may have to make adjustments. You do not want execute this change just prior to the placement of your business on the market.

In Jim Collins book, *Good to Great*, he uses the bus analogy to say (my paraphrase):

- Get the right people on the bus
- Get the wrong people off the bus
- Get everyone in the right seats
- Get the bus headed in the right direction

You need to go through the process right now in order to determine if you have the right team with the right roles.

Andrew Carnegie once said, "The secret of success is not in doing your own work but in recognizing the right man to do it."

Delegation

The delegation of some key management duties will be needed. Your key leaders should be able to demonstrate their ability in order to ensure leadership in the following areas:

- Sales & Marketing
- Financial Management
- Human Resources
- Operations

Stephen W. Comiskey said, "*You can delegate authority, but not responsibility.*" While you begin to pass on some responsibility to your team and when you try to sell your business, you are ultimately responsible and will suffer the most if unsuccessful. Do not micromanage but ensure you have regular meetings to verify if performance goals and action plans are met.

A simple delegation rule is the acronym SMART. It is a quick checklist for proper delegation. Delegated tasks must be:

- Specific
- Measurable
- Agreed
- Realistic
- Time bound

Begin to determine who you will delegate key responsibilities to. Next, I will discuss how you can ensure they are right for the roles and responsibilities you will delegate.

Leadership Assessments

An assessment of the skills your management team possesses is important in the early stages of a plan to sell your business. There are many effective tools available to help in this process. My company can provide web-based leadership assessments, if you have difficulty finding that service in your area.

I will provide you a simple tool to jumpstart the process if you would like. If you have the resources, consider having a professional 360° assessment performed.

The following is a simple assessment you can fill out on each leader to begin the process of determining where the gaps are in their skills and create a plan to fill them. Rank your key employee on each of the following questions. The ranking scale is as follows:

1 - Poor 2- Fair 3 - Average 4- Good 5 - Outstanding

Question	1	2	3	4	5
Sets priorities well					
Exhibits a positive mental attitude					
Open to change					
Delegates to other well					
Takes responsibility well (not a blame shifter)					
Set business/department goals					
Develops clear plans and activities well					
Problem-solving capabilities					
Communicates well with others					
Upholds our mission, vision and values					
Dedication to customer satisfaction					
Dedication to quality of product or service					
Careful about controlling costs and overhead					
Works well with all departments					
Is a process thinker					
Organized and efficient					
Time management skills					
Willingness to go the extra mile					
Assertive when appropriate					
Reliable and constant					

Recognizes the contributions of others					
Trustworthiness					
Motivates others					
Listens well					
High ethical standards					
Represents the company well					
Fosters collaboration					
Ability to learn					
Knowledge of all operations					
Evaluates employees performance					
Sets high standers for others to follow					
Presents plans and proposals well					
Coaches employees					
Treats others with dignity and respect					
Displays tolerance and flexibility					
Goal setting					
Encourages growth in others					
Honesty					
Fairness					
Results orientated					
Totals					

Total the number in each column. A good manager should rank high on three's, four's and five's and have few one's and two's. Look at the one's and two's and determine how that behavior can improve. Develop an action plan to move this key employee from where they are to where they need to be for the type of role they perform.

You may want to copy it and ask others to score the same individual; you may be surprised how different peers and even employees may see them, which is why 360° Assessments are valuable and effective. As I accentuated earlier, we all become too close to our business and may lack objectivity.

If you would like to have a digital copy of the survey above go to: http://businessforsaleblueprint.com/book-resources

Professionally done Leadership Assessments

If possible, I highly recommend having Leadership Assessments professionally performed.

The testing service I use describes a person's World View and Self-View. It provides graphs of abilities in the following areas:

- Critical leadership/management skills
- Human resource management
- Performance management
- Planning and organizing
- Production management
- Self management
- Leadership by example
- Guiding vision
- Inspiring excellence

Contact me if you would like information on obtaining the assessment I recommend.

Leadership Development Program

Once you are armed with information about the skills, attitudes, and abilities of your key leaders, you must now create a Leadership Development Program to help them in areas of weakness.

Discuss with each employee the results from whatever mechanism you used to determine areas of improvement. Obtain their agreement on what should be worked on first and then agree on how to accomplish the needed improvements.

The following are a few ideas:

Enroll employee(s) in a Leadership Training Program
Investigate what training options are available in your area. A couple of nationally recognized leadership training programs are offered by Dale Carnegie and internationally by LMI (Leadership Management Institute). Many state and community colleges also offer excellent leadership training programs.

Books and Audio Programs
Purchase books or audios on the subject the employee needs to improve. Ask them to write a report on what they learned and how they plan to apply it. Follow-up with them every three months and ask them to provide you specific examples of how they applied the new skill.

On-Line Training
There are many on-line programs that can be used to help employees improve in areas of weakness.

I have partnered with a national expert in employee testing and training. They provide hundreds of online classes (most offering Continuing Education Units) that can target each employee's specific areas where improvement is desired.

If you would like to be connected with this source contact me.

Hire an Executive Coach to work with them
You may want to consider hiring an Executive Coach to work closely with your key employees. Executive Coach's can perform the following tasks:

- Be a mentor
- Help develop needed leadership skills
- Hold the employee accountable for goal performance
- Provide you with feedback
- Free you up on improving the business
- Provide coaching skills you may not possess
- Time efficient for employees (often done over the phone)
- Close the gaps between where the employee is now and where they need to be

Many Executive Coaches will provide their own assessment survey tools to help them know how to best assist their client.

There are more and more people who perform executive management coaching so be careful; hire a reputable organization and verify their references thoroughly.

Management Team Retention

Keeping key leaders before and after the sale is essential. With our awareness of how important it is to have a management team that can run operations when you are gone, you must develop a strategy that will not only keep these key employees, but also enables them to help increase the value of the business at the same time.

Key Leader Incentive Bonus Plan

Incentive plans for your key leaders must be designed to support your business transition goals; your desire is that they are seen as an asset to your company. There are many different strategies and formulas you can utilize to develop an incentive plan; however, consult with trusted advisors before implementing any plan. A poorly designed plan can be worse than no plan.

Successful Incentive Bonus

What makes a good incentive plan for the purposes of selling your business in the not-too-distant future? The incentive plan must include the following:

- Tied to specific performance metrics the employee has influence on
- Clearly documented and communicated
- Formulas and numbers are trusted by employees
- Ties the employee to the business over time
- Big enough for their eyes to light up and significantly impact income

Example Incentive Bonus Plan

Bob owns a manufacturing business that has averaged an EBITA of $400,000 over the last two years. He has identified two employees that he feels are critical to the successful sale of the business. One is the Director of Operations (Bill) and the other is the Business Manager (Sue). He creates an Incentive Plan that will pay Bill and Sue 25% bonus on the EBITA that is generated above $500,000. They now have a substantial incentive to help Bob grow the number that will greatly increase the sell price of the business. In one year, the business earns $700,000 in EBITA.

The plan will pay a bonus of $50,000 that is shared between Bill and Sue, each receiving $25,000.

Bob's plan is to pay 50% of the bonus in cash and the balance in a Non-Qualified Deferred Compensation plan with five year vesting. Bill and Sue each receive $12,500 now and know they will receive the balance over the five year period. The following is the outcome of this plan:

5 YEAR VESTING SCHEDULE

Year 1	0%
Year 2	20%
Year 3	40%
Year 4	60%
Year 5	100%

Notice this vesting plan is weighted to encourage them to stay to the fifth year. You and your advisors can design the schedule. Each year additional bonuses are incorporated into the plan with a new vesting plan for each contribution. This builds up and makes it difficult for a key employee to walk away and leave that money on the table.

Non-Qualified Deferred Compensation – (NQDC)

NQDC indicates the compensation that has been earned by an employee but has not yet been received from the employer. Because the ownership of the compensation, which may be monetary or otherwise, has not been transferred to the employee, it is not yet part of the employee's earned income and is not counted as taxable income.

Be sure to work with a trusted financial advisor and attorney to help you set up a NQDC plan. There are legal issues that have to be addressed, such as Forfeiture Agreements.

Stay Bonus

Another incentive option you could consider is a Stay Bonus. This is more directly linked to the sale of your business. Like the Incentive Bonus, this bonus is designed to make it difficult for a key leader to leave after the sale of the business. The following should be some of your objectives:

- Keep key employees through the sale and transfer of ownership
- Reward key employees for their help on your achievement of performance results that increased the value of the business
- Assure the buyer that key employees are provided incentives to continue and help in the transition

The following are some Stay Bonus ideas:

- Offer a percentage of the sale price to be included in the bonus pool
- Key managers should be entitled to a prorated share as they are vested
- Three year vesting period. One third at closing, one third after one year, and balance after two years.

This plan should also be drafted and reviewed by your attorney. You will also need to set up an escrow account for the funds to be distributed from.

Non-Compete Agreements

It is amazing how many businesses do not have Non-Compete Agreements (NCA) with their key employees. Employees who have been with you for a while without a NCA will likely balk at signing one now. An NCA is very important for the protection of the value of your business.

If during the negations with a buyer you lost a key employee and they took some key customers with them, how would it affect the deal? You are right, it would likely kill it completely or the buyer will return with a much lower offer.

The following is what you want an NCA to perform:

- Tie the employee to your company (reduce the likelihood of going to or becoming a competitor)
- Reassures your potential buyer that key employees will not leave and take clients or employees with them

Again you need an attorney and trusted advisor to help you create a strong, legally binding NCA. Many NCA's are unenforceable unless they provide fair compensation for signing the agreement.

You may tie the NCA with one of your incentive plans. No NCA, no bonus plan.

Are they enforceable?
The following is a quote from Attorney Neil E. Klingshirn:

"Generally speaking, yes. Courts have traditionally frowned upon restrictions placed by employers on their employees' right to find and make a living. However, courts will enforce non-competition agreements if:

- *The employer proves that it has a legitimate business interest to protect by restricting its employees' right to compete against it*
- *The restriction on the employee's right to compete is no greater than that necessary to protect the employer's business interest*
- *The covenant not to compete is supported by consideration, meaning that the employee received something in exchange for it"*

Enforcing Noncompete Agreements

Noncompete agreements can be hard to enforce. Many courts perceive them as attempts to limit an individual's ability to obtain employment. For that reason, most courts will insist that a noncompete agreement be reasonably limited in geographic scope and duration. To ensure that your noncompete clause or agreement is enforceable:

- Have your agreement drafted by your attorney
- Make sure that it follows applicable state law
- Be sure there is sufficient consideration (i.e., compensation) given to the employee for signing the agreement. If the agreement is part of the hiring process, giving the employee the job is sufficient consideration for agreeing to refrain from competing later on
- Have it drawn as narrowly as possible
- Define the company's legitimate or protectable interest
- Reasonably relate the restrictions to what the company seeks to protect
- Structure the agreement with an eye toward partial enforcement
- Do not selectively utilize or enforce such agreements

Action Items

❑ *Determine the roles and responsibilities you will begin to delegate*

❑ *Perform an evaluation of the skills and weaknesses of your key leaders.*

❑ *Consider hiring an Executive Coach to work with key employees*

❑ *Develop an incentive plan that ties key leaders to the organization and helps in the sale of the business*

- ❑ *Talk with your Attorney about the creation of Non-Compete Agreements for key employees*
- ❑ *List actions you plan to take on your Action List Worksheet (or Action Planning tool you selected) and set the appropriate dates and steps you plan to take*

Chapter 5
Customer Base

In this chapter, I will discuss several critical areas related to your customers. These critical areas are as follow:

- Customer Diversity
- Customer Analysis
- Customer Retention
- Customer Satisfaction
- Customer Relationship Management (CRM)
- Sales Growth Strategy

Buyer's Perspective

All your cash flow (the primary value of your business) comes from your customers. The prospective buyer of your business will be considering the following:

- *Will sales projections (used to establish business value) continue as planned*
- *Is the company's reputation with clients solid and will it continue after the purchase*
- *What is the risk of losing key customers*
- *Is there a Sales Growth Plan*
- *Will the loss of a few key clients place the company in extreme jeopardy*
- *Are critical customer relationships limited to the business owner*

If you have any hope of selling for a premium price, your buyer must believe they can continue or even exceed your current sales trends. If they do not believe it, they will not pay you for it

Customer Diversity
Do you have any clients who are over 10% of total sales? 20%? 50%?

If you have any major clients who are a large percentage of your overall sales and profit, you are at risk of having the value of your business greatly discounted. Between now and the time you begin the process of selling your business, you must accomplish the following:

- Reduce the dependency on your major clients by recruiting new clients

- Reduce the risk of losing a large client

I will discuss each of these in detail.

Plan for Recruiting New Clients
To make the larger clients a smaller percentage of sales and profits (thereby reducing risk), you must make new client recruitment one of your primary goals. I will discuss how to develop a Growth Plan but now consider the following:

- Make this a written goal
- Place it where everyone can see it
- Discuss it regularly with employees
- Develop a list of 20 possible ways you can achieve the goal
- Take action (incorporate them on your actions plans)

Reduce Big Client Risk

Losing the big customer will always be viewed as a risk by a potential buyer but there are strategies you can use to help the buyer feel a little more comfortable. The following are potential ideas or strategies:

- Explore if you can develop some sort of long term contract that is beneficial to you and the customer
- Document their satisfaction level from letters, emails, and surveys
- Make sure client works well with multiple employees and is not there just because of the relationship established with one or two people
- Hold meetings with your clients key buyer's and decision makers every six months and ask the following questions:
    - How are we doing?
    - What can we do better?
    - What changes do you see coming in your company or industry?
    - How do we compare with the best perceived alternative (your competitors)?

Obtain Expert Advice

There are many sources of great books, trainers, and consultants that specialize in sales and marketing. Your situation is likely to be unique and may require a tailored solution for your business or industry.

Customer Base Analysis

At this point in the preparation process, you need to carefully analyze your customer base. It is amazing how little most business owners know about their customers. It is very important that you really "KNOW" your customer, why they buy, how they buy, and will they continue to buy. The following is some information you want to discover:

- Each customer's percentage of sales

- Each customer's profit margin
- Customer retention percentage
- Customers Lost
- Customers Won
- Customer sales comparisons year over year
- Average invoice amount
- Average profit per order per customer
- Bid opportunities per customer
- Bids lost per customer
- Customer demographics
- Customer psychographics
- Customer travel distance
- Customer segmentation
- Lifetime value
- How acquired
- 80/20 Analysis (20% of your customers likely do 80% of you sales and profit)
- Satisfaction level
- Buying preferences

The above list barely scratches the surface of what you could learn about your customers. Demonstrating to a potential buyer how much you know your client is impressive and helpful in the sale process.

Customer Retention

Customer Retention is the activities you take to reduce customer defections.

Customer Retention was mentioned earlier but I would like to discuss it further. It is critical that you have a strategy to retain customers. In most business, the cost of customer acquisition is very high and yet few companies have a plan to retain customers. Some customer attrition is unavoidable with issues, such as economic slowdowns, business need changes, and even closings that are beyond your control.

Customer delight

You must make the effort to delight your customers. The best way to do that is to exceed customer expectations. You cannot develop a strategy to delight your customers if you do not clearly understand the customer's expectations.

Customers have similar basic expectations such as; product quality, competitive pricing, service responsiveness, appearance of facilities and staff.

Kano's customer delight model

Take the time to study the Kano Model as you develop your strategy to increase your customers delight. The basic concept of the Kano Model is that what customers once thought was exceptional will become the norm. You must make the effort to stay ahead of the customers' expectations and find new ways to delight them. If you don't, your competitor will.

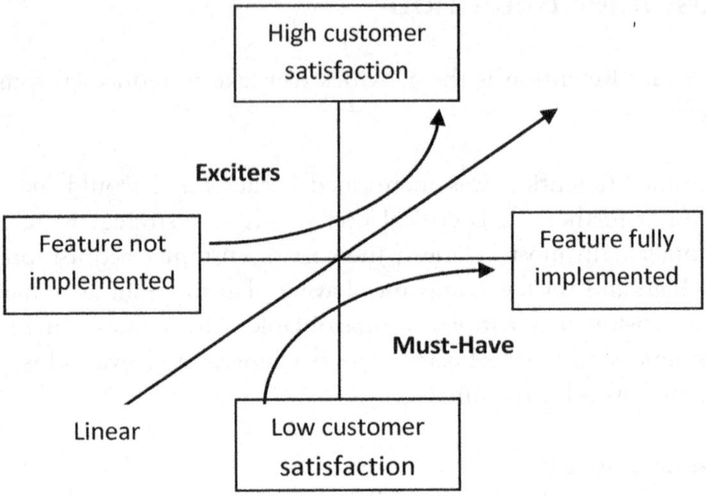

Kano Model

Over time, as customers experience delight, their expectations change. What was exceptional becomes the norm. In Kano's terms, what used to be an attractive attribute becomes a linear or basic attribute. It no longer delights. Delight decays into normal expectation, and companies have to look for new ways to pleasantly surprise customers. In a competitive environment, it seems to make little sense to resist the quest for customer delight because competitors will simply drive up expectations anyway.

Customer Desertion

The opposite of retention is desertion or defection. Some of the causes of customer desertion are:

- Failure to meet expectations (or delight) in quality or service
- Poor customer complaint handling
- Rude or discourteous employees
- Taking the customer for granted
- Failure to communicate with customer

Customer Retention Metrics

The following are recommendations for establishing benchmarks and baselines measurement for customer retention.

- Set a retention goal and monitor closely your results.

- Remember the Pareto principle. Recognize that 20% of the customers contribute to 80% of the profits, or which 20% of the causes are resulting in 80% of the complaints or desertion, etc.

- Use absolute numbers as well as percentages. The percentage, being relative, must be supplemented with the factual value in numbers (e.g., indicate that a 15% desertion is the equivalent 3,500 customers).

- Allow one year for your customers to return before considering them desertions.

- Use neutral parties to conduct research instead of your staff.

Customer Satisfaction

I discussed the importance of Customer Satisfaction in Client Retention. Following, I will discuss how to determine the level of satisfaction by utilizing a survey tool. I recommend performing an annual formal survey and creating a method to obtain a minimum of monthly customer satisfaction trends.

Customer Surveys

You have two choices:

- Build your own survey tool and implement it yourself

- Hire a professional survey firm to conduct the survey for you

The only advantage to do it yourself is to save money, and I believe hiring a firm that specializes in customer surveys has several advantages as indicated below:

- They have the experience
- They likely have built an automated survey tool
- Your results can be compared to others in their database (the biggest advantage)

I will share with you how to conduct your own survey and provide you with some sample questions. You can design a survey with your own questions that fit with some special areas you may want to learn about your clients.

Customer Survey Questions

The first challenge is selecting the necessary set of questions to ask your customers. The whole purpose of the survey is to learn what areas they may have some level of dissatisfaction in order for you to improve in that area.

The following is a sample survey with some generic questions that you will want to start with and then develop further. Some may not be relevant to your industry and can be eliminated. This survey uses the Likert five point scale:

1 – Very Dissatisfied
2 – Somewhat Dissatisfied
3 – Neutral
4 – Satisfied
5 – Extremely Satisfied

Question	1	2	3	4	5
Friendly and courteous staff					
Knowledgeable competent staff					

Estimate response time					
Delivery when promised (meets deadlines)					
Reasonable pricing					
Understanding of client needs					
Quality of product/service					
Clear and helpful quotes and proposals					
Accurate invoicing					
Shipments meet order specifications					
Range of capabilities/products/services					
Staying current with industry needs					
Responsiveness to problems or complaints					
Response time to your communications					
Overall satisfaction with our organization					

You want to also include open-ended questions that provide additional and valuable information. You can design your own but the following are some examples and ideas:

- What products or services would you like for us to add?
- What is the one task we can implement that would most increase your satisfaction?
- Would you recommend us to others? Why or why not?
- Do you plan to buy from us in the next six months? Why or why not?

Tabulating the Score

A great way to calculate your survey score is to compile the data into a spreadsheet with a column for each participating company and then average the scores. Convert the averages into a percentage by multiplying the average by 20.

Example:

Question	1	2	3	4	5	Avg	Score
Friendly and courteous staff	4	3	3	5	3	3.6	72%
Knowledgeable competent staff	3	2	4	3	4	3.2	64%

Customer Focus Group

An effective way to obtain more from your survey is to pull together customers for a focus group. This will help you better understand the results and at the same time demonstrate to your customers how important the survey is to you and your desire to improve.

Bring together five to eight clients for a lunch meeting and share with them the survey results. Next, ask them to provide you with feedback on all the weak scores. For example: Why is our staff not perceived as knowledgeable as they received only a 64% score? You will leave with some great ideas on how to improve your satisfaction level and an improved relationship with some key clients.

Ongoing Satisfaction Measuring Program

In addition to an annual survey, you must also have a mechanism in place to measure satisfaction in smaller intervals than annually. Weekly is ideal but at least monthly indicators are needed. Be creative and brainstorm with your employees on how you can measure customer satisfaction on a frequent basis. Below is a list of what some businesses have implemented:

- Comment card satisfaction rating with each shipment
- Email survey to clients after each shipment using an online tool, such as Survey Monkey
- Call clients with prepared questions
- Random sampling mailed surveys to clients each month

Regardless of the tool you decide you utilize, you need to remember the following:

- Be consistent

- Assign one person responsible to collect the data
- Compile the data into a satisfaction score
- Report score to entire staff each month
- Set an improvement goal
- Have meetings and discussions on how to improve
- Stay alert for trends that are going the wrong direction
- If trends are going the wrong way, jump on it fast and solve the problems that caused a decline in satisfaction

Customer Relationship Management (CRM)
I believe that the use of some sort of CRM system is needed to properly interact with clients and prospects. CRM is an integrated information system that is used to plan, schedule, and control the presales and post sales activities in an organization. CRM embraces all aspects of dealing with prospects and customers, including the call center, sales force, marketing, technical support, and field service.

The primary goal of CRM is to improve long-term growth and profitability through a better understanding of customer behavior. CRM aims to provide more effective feedback and improved integration to better gauge the return on investment (ROI) in these areas.

I will not discuss CRM extensively in this chapter, but I primarily desire to encourage you to be certain your business gathers adequate data on clients and prospects.

Many years ago Harvey McKay developed what he called the McKay 66. There were 66 questions he wanted his sales representatives to discover from each prospect. This information helps them better understand each client and tailor sales approaches to their needs. If you would like more information on McKay 66, go to Harvey Mackay's website http://www.harveymackay.com/tools/ and download his entire list.

I had a client simplify this to 26 questions that they wanted their sales team to learn about their clients. Create your own list and start gathering information about your clients.

Sales Growth Strategy

Now that you are working on keeping your customers and making them more satisfied, I want to focus our attention toward finding many new clients. This is your Growth Strategy.

Many business brokers I have spoken with consider this to be one of the most important "value drivers" next to cash flow. It is difficult to sell a business whose sales are trending downward. This is why a fully developed and deployed Growth Strategy is so important.

The following are three primary methods on increasing sales:

1. Sell your current products/services to more customers

2. Sell more products/services to current customers

3. Raise prices on the current products/services that the business sells to current customers

I recommend you analyze all three of these strategies. For the purposes of making your big clients a smaller and smaller percentage of sales, I will focus on the following:

"GET MORE CUSTOMERS"

There are a lot of great resources out there to help you find and attract more clients; I will not try to tell you how. Besides, each industry has a unique client base that may require different strategies. However, the following are some general ideas:

- Know your target prospect including demographics and psychographics
- Develop a list of prospects that fit that model
- Create multiple mechanisms to let those prospects know what you offer
- Know your Unique Selling Proposition
- Make sure someone in your organization is accountable for new client generation
- Bring in experts to help in the training if that core skill is not within your organization
- Create a written Sales and Marketing Plan

Action Items

- ❑ *Establish a Customer Diversity Goal*
- ❑ *Create a detailed analysis of your customers*
- ❑ *Create a Retention Plan*
- ❑ *Regularly measure Customer Satisfaction*

- ☐ *Analyze your CRM and develop a process to capture valuable information about your customers and prospects*
- ☐ *Develop a written Growth Strategy plan to "Get More Customers" and execute that plan*
- ☐ *List actions you plan to take on your Action List Worksheet (or Action Planning tool you selected) and set the appropriate dates and steps you plan to take*

Chapter 6
Performance Metrics

In this chapter, I will discuss the numbers of your business.

Definition: *Metrics are a set of measurements that quantify results. Performance metrics quantify performance. Project metrics tell you whether the project is meeting its goals. Business metrics define the business' progress in measurable terms.*

Buyer's Perspective

The buyer will want to analyze your numbers and determine:

- *How do you compare with the industry?*
- *How do you compare with competitors (where data is possible)?*
- *How you compare with your past results (are you improving)?*
- *How you capture and monitor your metrics?*

If you can demonstrate good results on the questions above, you will position yourself in the elite class of professional businesses.

Key Performance Indicators

The first tasks you must analyze are your Key Performance Indicators (KPI). KPIs are the measurements that best reflect the critical success factors of your organization. Each company and particularly each industry may have different KPIs. You and your management/leadership team must select KPIs that best reflect success in your company. KPIs must ensure the following:

- Reflect your company's goals
- Must be key to your company's success
- Must be quantifiable (measurable)

While you have to determine your own KPIs, I can provide some idea generation with some typical KPIs found in many companies. The following are examples that will be a good place to begin:

Sales and Marketing Sample Key Performance Indicators

- Sales increase of same period previous year
- Monthly Gross Profit
- Monthly Value Added
- Customer Retention
- Customer Defection
- Bid Win/Loss Ratio
- Sales calls per rep
- Incoming customer orders
- Average order size
- Number of estimates per day
- Presentations per month
- Prospecting calls per week

Human Resources Sample Key Performance Indicators

- Percentage of new employee retention after x time
- Employee turnover percentage
- Percentage job offer acceptance rate
- New employee satisfaction rate with recruiting process
- Percentage of vacancies filled within x time
- Average Number of Interviews from Submitted applications
- Recruitment source ratio - internal -v- external applicants

- Recruiting fee as percentage of annual salary
- Percentage of new employees with a recruiting fee paid
- Performance evaluation scores on hired candidates after, a given period
- Average time that transpires from the moment a candidate is submitted to a hiring manager to receiving initial feedback from the hiring manager
- Average cost to recruit per job position
- Average open time of job positions
- Average number of responses for open job positions
- Average number of interviewees for open job positions within a given measurement period.
- Average time to recruit

Employee Development

- Percentage of employees receiving regular performance and career development reviews
- Average time employees are in the same job or function
- Percentage of new hire retention after a given period
- Ratio of internal versus external training (hours or cost)
- Employee satisfaction with training
- ROI of training
- Percentage of Human Resources budget spent on training.
- Percentage of employees gone through training in a given period
- Average number of training hours per employee
- Average training costs per employee

Finance and business Key Performance Indicators

- Accounting costs
- Accounts Payable

- Accounts Payable Turnover
- Accounts Receivable Collection Period
- Accounts Receivable Turnover
- Average value of overdue invoices
- Cash Flow Return on Investments (CFROI) The list below contains factors which while important may or may not become key performance measures - it will all depend on the objectives of the organization at a given point in time
- Common Stock Equity
- Corporate credit rating
- Cost Income Ratio
- Cost per pay slip issued
- Creditor days
- Cumulative Annual Growth Rate (CAGR)
- Cycle time for expense reimbursements
- Cycle time to perform periodic close
- Cycle time to process payroll
- Cycle time to resolve an invoice error
- Cycle time to resolve payroll errors
- Days Payable
- Debtor days
- Direct costs
- EBIT (Earnings before Interest and Taxes)
- EBITDA (Earnings before Interest, Taxes, Depreciation and Amortization)
- Enterprise Value / Takeover Value
- Equity ratio
- Fixed costs
- Indirect costs
- Invoicing processing costs
- Long-Term Debt
- Marginal costs
- Net Change in Cash
- Number of invoices outstanding
- Number of overdue invoices

- Other Current Liabilities
- Other Non-current Liabilities
- Payment errors as Percentage of total payroll disbursement
- Percentage of bad debts against invoiced revenue
- Percentage of electronic invoices
- Percentage of expense report exception line items
- Percentage of financial reports issued on time
- Percentage of invoices disputed
- Percentage of invoices requiring special payment
- Percentage of low value invoices
- Percentage of manual payroll payments
- Preferred Stock Equity
- Profit per customer
- Profit per employee
- Profit per product
- Profit per project
- Receivables against Product,
- Region, Sales office
- Return on capital employed (ROCE)
- Return on Equity (ROE)
- Short-Term Debt
- Total Assets
- Total Current Liabilities
- Total Equity
- Total Liabilities
- Total sum of monetary value of outstanding invoices
- Total value of overdue invoices
- Variable costs

Health and Safety - Sample Key Performance Indicators

- Health and safety prevention costs within the month
- Lost time (in hours) due to accidents (including fatalities) per e.g. 100,000 hours worked

- Lost time (in hours) due to non-fatal accidents per e.g. 100,000 hours worked
- Number of non-conformance with legal or internal standards in safety inspections
- Number of reportable accidents per e.g. 100,000 hours worked (including fatalities)
- Number of reportable non-fatal accidents per e.g. 100,000 hours worked
- Number of solved safety non-conformances for the month
- Percentage of attendance at occupational health and safety (OHS) committee meetings
- Percentage of corrective actions closed out within specified time-frame
- Percentage of fatal accidents relative to all accidents (non-fatal and fatal) per e.g. 100,000 hours worked
- Percentage of occupational health and safety (OHS) committee recommendations implemented
- Percentage of products/services assessed for health & safety impacts
- Percentage of significant products and services categories subject to procedures in which health and safety impacts of products and services are assessed for improvement
- Percentage of staff with adequate Occupational Health and Safety (OHS) training
- Total of hours in safety and health training in the month

Environmental Key Performance Indicators

- Amount of energy saved due to conservation and efficiency improvements.
- Average electrical consumption per employee or product sold
- CO2 (Carbon dioxide) or VOC (Volatile Organic Compound) Tons per employee per month
- Energy costs per unit of production

- Energy saved due to conservation & efficiency improvements
- Greenhouse gas (GHG) emissions per employee per month
- Number of paper pages used per employee per month
- Percentage of hazardous operational waste
- Percentage of materials used that are recycled input materials
- Percentage of non-hazardous operational waste
- Percentage of recycled hazardous operational waste
- Percentage of recycled non-hazardous operational waste
- Total energy used per unit of production
- Total on-site created energy
- Total Purchased Energy per month
- Waste disposed of per amount of product manufactured
- Water use per employee per month
- Water used per amount of product manufactured

Manufacturing Sample Key Performance Indicators

- Parts Six Sigma Level
- Production throughput
- Employee hours per part
- Daily defects
- Monthly Cost of Quality (by department and company)
- Scraped material pounds/dollars
- 5S Department Score
- Equipment downtime/uptime
- Equipment maintenance hours

While this is a comprehensive list, it still may not include the KPIs for your business. The following are my recommendations for creating your own list of KPIs:

Select three to eight KPIs from each category that apply to your business

- Analyze the past three year history for each metric
- Establish new goals based on improving past results
- Benchmark with top companies in your industry
- Track these measures monthly
- Post KPIs in each department
- Create incentive plans related to KPI success
- Link KPIs to performance reviews

Industry Comparisons

As mentioned earlier, a potential buyer will want to know how you compare with others. They will want to buy a company that is preferably in the top 25% of the industry, maybe even the top 10%. You must be proactive and know where you are in comparison to others and illustrate this with pride to your prospective buyer.

You can be assured that one of the first key points a prospective buyer will analyze is how you stack up against others in your industry. When you or the buyer obtains a certified business valuation, the valuation expert will conduct industry comparisons as a part of the valuation process.

The following are some sources where you can obtain your industry comparisons:

Trade Associations

Many Trade Associations provide this service for their membership. They will likely perform an annual survey of the members asking them all standard questions. Most of these comparisons will involve financial issues with metrics, such as Gross Profit, Inventory Turns, Net Profit, and/or Financial Ratios among others. Verify with your Trade Association to discover what is available.

Banker

Your banker (Business Loan Officer) will likely have access to your industry metrics by SIC (Standard Industrial Classification) code.

They use this information when they review your financial statements to evaluate how you are performing. Work closely with your banker and ask them to show you the numbers they compare you with and discuss where he/she feels you should be. Ask for a copy of these metrics and use it to establish goals in order to place you in the upper tier of your industry.

Purchase Industry Report

There are sources available online to order industry reports. One example is www.hovers.com, which is a Dunn & Bradstreet company. Search for a reputable source that you can trust.

Peer Groups

Many associations help form peer groups that you can work with to compare numbers. Many times these groups are formed with similar businesses from other parts of the country to avoid competitive issues. If your association does not have one, you could establish your own. Conduct a search on the web and you will find many sources for advise and even companies in the business that organize Peer Groups together (for a fee of course).

Find a source and ensure you are near or at the top of your industry.

Benchmarking

Benchmarking is related to industry comparisons that I just discussed, but it consists of more valuable information and insights for improving your business. Benchmarking is the process that determines who is the very best, who sets the standard, and what that standard is.

Benchmarking Process

Following are some general recommendations on benchmarking your business, process or procedure.

- Clearly define the process, metric or procedure you want to benchmark
- Identify potential benchmarking partners
- Identify sources for collecting data
- Collect data from your benchmarking partners (visit when possible)
- Determine the gap between your results and the "Best in Class"
- Determine why there is a gap
- Set goals for future performance
- Communicate goals to all employees
- Review results
- Follow a process improvement methodology to move to desired goals

The advantage of this type of benchmarking is that you may decide to venture outside your industry and find "World Class" processes that no one in your industry uses. This can provide you with a competitive advantage by applying innovations that impact your business in many key areas.

Action Items

- ❑ *Work with your leadership team to establish your company's KPIs*
- ❑ *Find out how your metrics compare with leaders in your industry*
- ❑ *Benchmark with companies who have "World Class" processes*
- ❑ *List on your Action List Worksheet (or Action Planning tool you selected) and set the appropriate dates and steps you plan to take*

Chapter 7
Workplace Organization

In this chapter, I will discuss the overall appearance of your business. I know the old saying "don't judge a book buy it cover," but the truth is, your business will be judged by its appearance. It is natural that a potential buyer who assesses his or her perspective business will have doubts if they see disorganization and clutter.

A clean, organized, and efficient facility will help attract a premium price for your business.

Buyer's Perspective

- *The buyer will want to buy a business that has the appearance of success*
- *The buyer may still be interested (if the numbers look good) but expect them to offer a much lower multiple. They will battle for a bargain price if the business does not have the optimum appearance*

5S Tool for Workplace Organization

The best tool that I have found for creating the ideal workplace organizational structure is one that comes from Japan. I will focus on how 5S can transform the appearance and organization of your business.

The Benefits of 5S

Benefits for the Employees are as follow:

1. A more pleasant work environment
2. More satisfying jobs
3. Process that makes the job easier
4. A process that makes sense
5. Pride in the workplace
6. Employee and customer respect
7. Positive mental attitude

5S simply creates a better place to work

Benefits for the company:

Higher quality, lower costs, easier maintenance, greater customer satisfaction, and higher profitability

1. Sales
2. Savings
3. Safety
4. Standardization
5. Satisfaction

5S can be the foundation for other continuous Improvement processes

The term 5S actually comes from five Japanese words that start with "S" that we have Americanized by finding 5 English words with similar meanings that also begin with "S." The following are the original Japanese words and their meaning:

- ***Seiri*** **(Sort)** - To remove what is not needed and keep what is needed

- ***Seiton* (Straighten)** - Place items in such a way that they can be easily reached whenever they are needed.

- ***Seiso* (Shine)** - Keep work areas and equipment clean and polished; no trash or dirt

- ***Seiketsu* (Standardize)** - Maintain cleanliness after cleaning - perpetual cleaning

- ***Shitsuke* (Sustain)** - Commitment to inspire pride and adherence to standards established for the four components

You will often hear many companies speak of 6S. The added "S" word is Safety; I will not include it here but it is a natural addition. Safety is a byproduct of the 5S Strategy but it is fine if you want to include it and call it 6S.

I will discuss in detail each of these categories. There is a great deal of information available on the internet to help you further with your efforts to 5S your facility.

Not just for the plant or warehouse
If you implement 5S in your company, you need to ensure it is implemented throughout the entire company. The need may seem more obvious in the production facility or warehouse, but the need is likely just as great in the office. Make this process a task that all employees get involved in.

#1 Sort

***Seiri* - To remove what is not needed and keep what is needed.**

- Materials, tools, equipment, and supplies that are not frequently used should be moved to a separate, common storage area. Items that are not used should be discarded.

- Do not keep items just because they might be used, someday.

- "When in doubt throw it out"

- Sorting is the first step in making a work area tidy. It makes it easier to find the items you need and frees up additional space.

- Use a "Red Tag" Process for items that need a higher level approval, and move them to a holding area until evaluation. They may be stored or discarded.

- Separate needed from unneeded items.

- Leave only the bare essentials.
    - Remove unneeded items from the work area (red tag).
    - Remove all excess items from the work area.
    - Is it needed, in what quantities, and where should it be located?

- Hold excess items within the shop storage area for 14 days or less.

- Assign a person to organize and manage the shop storage area.

- Assign a person to organize and manage the consolidated storage area.

- Organize working/storage area, disposing of all items in red tag area in a predetermined time.

Organization reduces work flow problems, increases product quality and productivity, and improves communication.

RED TAG System

- Start the red tag process within a designated area (shop, storage area, warehouse, and so forth)
- Identify the red tag targets
- Set red tag criteria
- Make red tags
- Attach red tags
- Evaluate red tag items
- Document the results of the red tagged items

Contact me and I will send you a Red Tag sample.

#2 Straighten

***Seiton* - Place items in such a way that they can be easily reached whenever they are needed.**

In this step, you organize, arrange, and identify your items in a work area for the most efficient and effective retrieval and return to its proper place. The words "Simplify," "Systemize," or "Set in order" are sometimes used in this step.

You should ask yourself the following questions:

What do I need to do my job?

Where should I locate this item?

How many of this item do I need?

- Commonly used tools should be readily available.
- Storage areas, cabinets, and shelves should be properly labeled.
- Clean and paint floors to make it easier to spot dirt, waste materials and dropped parts and tools.
- Outline areas on the floor to identify work areas, movement lanes, storage areas, finished and product areas among others.
- Place shadows on tool boards, making it easy to quickly see where each tool belongs.
- In an office, provide bookshelves for frequently used manuals, books, and catalogs and all items should be labeled.

The primary objective in this step is:

A place for everything and everything in its place, with everything properly identified and labeled.

#3 Shine

Seiso **- Keep items clean and polished; no trash or dirt in the workplace.**

Once you have everything, from each individual work area up to your entire facility, sorted (cleaned up) and organized, you must maintain it in these conditions, which will require regular cleaning. Sometimes the word "Sweep" is used for this "S".

- Regular, usually daily, cleaning is needed or everything will return to prior conditions.

- Regular cleaning and inspection makes it easy to spot lubricant leaks, equipment misalignment, breakage, missing tools, and/or low levels of supplies.

- When done on a regular, frequent basis, inspection or cleaning generally will not require a lot of time and in the long run, it will most likely save time.

#4 Standardize

***Seiketsu* - Maintain cleanliness after cleaning - perpetual cleaning**

To ensure that the first three steps in your 5S program continue to be effective, the fourth step is to simplify and standardize.

One of the hardest steps is avoiding old work habits. It is easy to slip back into what you have done for years. That is what everyone is familiar with, and it feels comfortable.

- Use visual controls – make it obvious to spot when an item is out of place.

- Any easy way to make people aware and remind them of the standards is to use labels, signs, posters, and banners.

A picture is worth a thousand words

Over the years, I have composed a diverse collection of before and after 5S pictures. Contact me and I will be glad to send some to you. They truly help you visualize the effectiveness of this process.

#5 Sustain

Shitsuke **- Commitment to inspire pride and adherence to standards established for the four components**

This is the final and most difficult step to achieve. For some reason, objects and items in businesses (and homes) seem to gravitate back to disorder and chaos. Think of this step as sustaining the benefits you obtain from your 5S program.

Sometimes the term "Self-Discipline" is used for the "S" here. This is appropriate because discipline is truly required in order to keep items from returning to their original state.

I bet you have experienced most of these steps when you tackled your garage, closet, or desk. In a few weeks or months, they seem to return to the way they were. I believe that the best way to sustain the efforts of the first four steps is to create a formal system that monitors the results of your 5S program.

Create a 5S AUDIT TEAM that will conduct monthly audits
Arrange a cross-functional team of employees and train them in 5S procedures. Create a scoring system and have the Audit Team monthly audit and score departments and work areas. Many companies create a friendly competition with rewards and incentives for staying at a 5S level.

All your efforts will not "Stick" without follow-up. Do not expect that you can clean up, maintain items organized and labeled, and ask people to clean and inspect their areas every day ~ and then have everything continue to happen without any follow-up.

Regularly educate employees about how to maintain the 5S standards.

Help is on the Web

After a quick Google search for "5S Audit Checklist," you will obtain great samples to use as a basis to build your own.

Contact me and I will be glad to send you an effective 5S Audit Checklist.

Facility Appearance

When you apply the 5S principles to your entire facility, you will solve the majority of your appearance issues. I want to be sure that nothing is left out. Your goal should be to have your business appear "show-ready" at all times. Buyer's will assume a certain amount of cleanup will be done for them but it is embarrassing when the prospective buyer talks to an employee and are told it "never looks like this." Imagine how much better it is for a potential buyer to hear "it always looks like this."

The following are a few additional areas to explore:

- Clean bathrooms
- Exterior of facilities (paint, repairs, among others)
- Lawn maintenance
- Lobby/reception area (clean and recent reading material)
- Plants thriving and green
- Trash picked up in parking lot and adjacent facilities (even if not yours, it can reflect on you)

Once again, you have to assess the facilities from the buyer's perspective. If you cannot do it, find someone fresh to assess and discover issues you need to address.

Action Items

- ❑ *Arrange a team of employees and teach them the 5S principles*

- ❑ *Ask the team to "attack" a small area first in order to prepare them for a larger area*
- ❑ *Develop a plan for which areas of the business will go through the 5S process and set a date for each*
- ❑ *Involve and train all employees and hold them accountable for 5S results*
- ❑ *Create an Audit Team to monitor that your efforts are being sustained*
- ❑ *Create an Audit Worksheet with your own questions and scoring*
- ❑ *Analyze all aspects of your facilities and the impression they make*
- ❑ *List actions you plan to take on your Action List Worksheet (or Action Planning tool you selected) and set the appropriate dates and steps you plan to take*

Chapter 8
Systems Documentation

In this chapter, I want to discuss the importance of having all your processes and procedures documented in a formal system.

Buyer's Perspective

- *The buyer will want to know that all the knowledge of running the business does not leave when the owner leaves*

- *The prospective buyer will have more confidence in the purchase of a company that has captured and documented all their best practices*

Michel Gerber who wrote the book *E-Myth Revisited* (which I recommend every business owner read) discusses how important it is to create what he calls a "franchise prototype." He believes you should operate your business as if you planned to sell 5,000 franchises. Franchisors provide their franchisees an operations manual complete with minute details on how to perform every process and procedure; they leave nothing to chance for their franchisees. Franchisors have already tested the best way to perform every task and have documented the most effective way. You must to do the same with your business; document how you perform tasks in your company.

- It will help you train employees

- You will capture hard earned efforts to find the best way to perform tasks

- You will effectively impress a potential buyer
- Obsolete procedures will become obvious during this process
- Employees will be forced to think about the best way to perform tasks

The best place to start is with SOPs.

Standard Operating Procedures (SOPs)

A SOP or Standard Operating Procedure is best described as a set of instructions that cover operational processes and procedures that lend themselves to a set standard way of doing them.

How to write SOPs

The following are principle aspects of SOPs:

- Uniform
- Provide detailed work instructions
- Promote consistency, structure and control
- Readily available
- Regularly reviewed
- Version controlled
- Management approved

I recommend that you have employees write their own SOPs. Assign someone with the primary responsibility to review and keep all SOPs consistent. Ask each writer to work from a standard template that includes the following elements:

1. Purpose / Background
2. Scope
3. Prerequisites

4. Procedures
5. Roles & Responsibilities
6. Training
7. Monitoring Requirements
8. Record Management
9. References
10. Definitions

I will go into each of these in more detail.

Purpose / Background
This section should describe any relevant background information and a description of why the procedure or guidance is necessary, such as regulatory requirements.

Scope
This section should identify the intended audience and/or where the SOP may be relevant and specific operations covered by the SOP.

Prerequisites
This section should provide the information needed before proceeding with the listed procedure, which may include necessary tools, documents, and/or certifications.

Procedures
This section is a step-by-step outline of the methods used in order to meet the purpose.

Roles & Responsibilities
Key Personnel – clearly identify key personnel that will have a primary role in this SOP and list their responsibilities as it relates strictly to this SOP. If necessary, include any contact information. If the 'key personnel' roles have not been assigned, provide additional information about who can be in charge of the listed responsibility.
Training

This section should describe how to obtain information about any available training (i.e. web-based, classroom, training guides, among others)

Monitoring Requirements

This section should define the need, frequency, and methods of conducting required assessments and/or monitoring, such as physical analysis of a covered process or internal and/or external inspections.

Record Management

This section incorporates record management practices.

References

This section should list any additional resources that may be useful when procedures are performed.

- Standards - Regulatory references should be listed here.
- Other SOPs - SOPs referred to in any other section of this SOP should be listed here.
- Supplementary Documents - The title of any forms available or used in this procedure should be listed here. Any documents included in the appendices should also be included here.

Definitions

This section should highlight and define frequently used terms and provide additional and/or relevant information needed in order to use and understand this SOP.

SOP Tips

- Link SOP with Process Maps when possible
- Ensure titles match content
- Track changes
- Create master index
- Consider electronic system
- Appoint a document control person

- Develop in small cross functional groups
- Begin each work step with a verb...

  Retrieve, issue, record, document, etc.

SOP Things to Avoid

- Not too much detail but sufficient to train from
- Avoid trade/commercial names. If supplier changes, the SOP will not need revised
- Do not include forms in the body of the SOP. Reference form titles on form numbers
- Avoid wordiness or unnecessary details
- Do not start title with "Process" or "Procedure". This makes it difficult to find if all the titles are the same

SOP Numbering System

It is important that you establish at the beginning a simple and consistent numbering system that is followed by all writers in your company.

The following is an example of a numbering system for Fred Herbert Consulting Group:

- Start all with FHCG-SOP
- Next two characters indicate Department
- AC - Accounting
- SH - Shipping
- SL - Sales
- Next three characters for unique record number

FHCG-SOP-AC-100

Below is a sample header that should appear on each page and show pertinent information.

FredHerbert.com Standard Operating Procedures		SOP #:	FHCG-SOP-AC-100
		Revision #:	Initial
		Implementation Date:	03/30/09
Page #:	1 of 2	Last Review/Update:	06/1/09
SOP Owner:	Fred Herbert	Approval: Fred	President
SOP Title: Processing Accounts Receivable			

Key Processes

You may have hundreds of processes in your business, but the key processes are those high level areas that must be performed to sustain day to day operations.

The following are a couple of examples:

Accounting

- Month End Closing
- Handling incoming Accounts Receivable
- Preparing Bank Deposits
- Monthly Statement Processing
- Running Aged Payables reports
- Past Due Collections
- Credit Memo
- New Customer Entry
- Invoicing

Human Resources

- Employment Application Processing
- Termination procedure
- New Hire Orientation
- Job posting procedure
- Maintaining Training Records
- Payroll Processing

Sales and Marketing

- Customer Complaint Handling

- New Client Credit Approval process
- Lead Generation Process
- Incoming Order Handling
- Schedule Approval Process
- Client Estimate Process
- CRM Collection Process

Operations

- Monthly Equipment Maintenance Process
- Employee Time Card Submission
- Employee Accident Process and Procedure
- Employee Performance Review
- Waste/Scrap Collection Process
- Supplier Approval
- Equipment Setup Process
- Control of Documents
- Quality Inspection Process

List each department and brainstorm with your employees the Key Processes in each area.

What is a Process?

- A process is a series of actions or activities that are performed to achieve a desired output or result

- Every process has an input and an output

- All process outputs should be measurable

- Process mapping is a method used to gain awareness of an organization's procedures and analyze them to identify sources of:
    - errors
    - defects
    - inefficiencies

- A process map makes the process more visible and simpler to comprehend to all those involved in the process.

- Process maps can be constructed at both micro and macro levels, depending on the level or the degree of detailing.

Process Mapping

This is a great tool that can be performed in lieu of a full SOP or in conjunction with an SOP. I recommend you identify the key processes in your business and begin the creation of Process Maps for each of them.

There are a series of standard symbols used in Process Mapping that you need become familiar with. These symbols are available on Microsoft products like Word, Excel, and Visio. This becomes a standard language that helps everyone visualize the performance. I prefer Visio but you can also create effective Process Maps with Word and Excel. The following are a few common symbols:

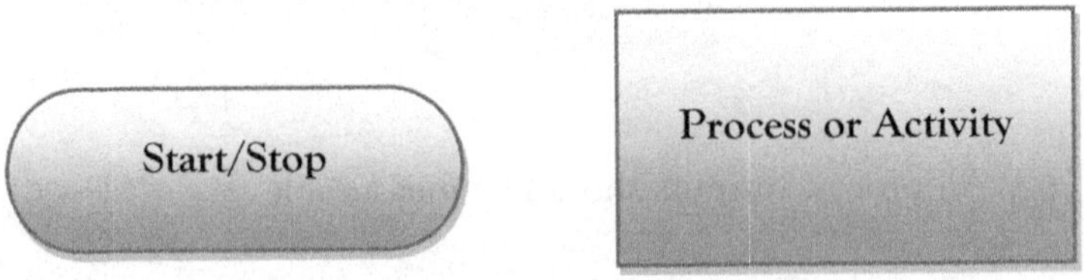

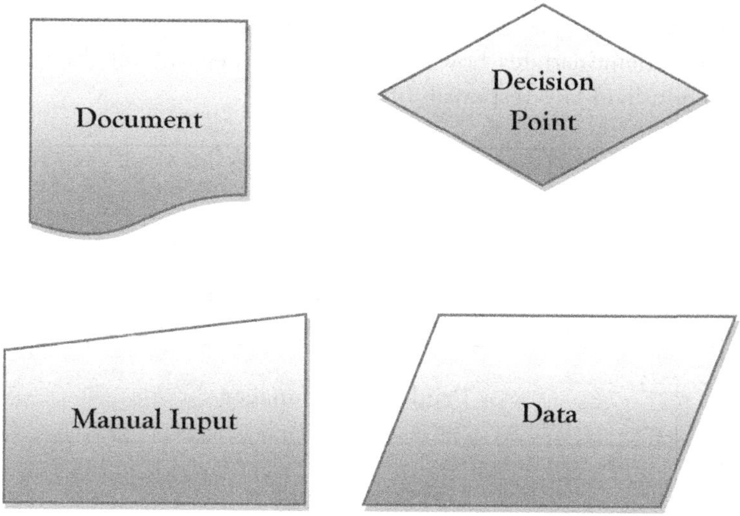

Connectors

Google "Process Maps" and you will obtain hundreds of great examples.

Deployment Maps

I highly recommend using Deployment Maps.

- This type of map illustrates activities within a function, job title, department, or other process participants.
- Often described as Swim Lanes.

See below an example of how a Deployment Process Map Works, which demonstrates how you might mix department duties with each individual's responsibilities.

Customer
Accounts Payable Clerk
Production Manager
Vendor/Supplier
Warehouse

Contact me and I will be glad to send you samples of deployment process maps I have done for clients.

On a side note, in two hours of meetings with a team of six employees at my client's office, we created a revised process the client calculated would save them over $17,000 per year in labor costs. This is a great example of how while you are building process maps, you can often indentify areas of improvement. While mapping, someone is bound to ask, "Why do we do it this way?" which is your opportunity to improve the process and save money immediately.

Now it is your turn; the following are some recommendations:

- Pull together a Process Mapping Team

- On a flip chart or white board, visualize and draw the process
- Be careful to keep it simple and stay away from unnecessary detail
- Analyze the details before including it on the computer
- Show the finished Process Map to someone unfamiliar with the process and see how well they understand it

Document Control System

All the effort of creating SOPs and Processes Maps can be wasted if you do not have a process to keep the documents current and make sure employees use the most current process. To manage this process you have to create a Document Control System.

ISO 9000 has a great model for controlling documents. In fact, Control of Documents should be one of your SOPs. The following is what ISO suggests the mandatory document control procedure must define:

- How you approve documents (e.g., procedures, flow-charts, process maps, etc.) prior to use (e.g., signed-off paper versions or added to your computer network via a password protected system)

- How you update and re-approve amended documents. Computer based systems are much easier to maintain

- How you identify changes (e.g. by date or issue number or by different fonts or colors)

- How you ensure that documents are available where they are needed

- How you control documents of external origin

- How you prevent the inadvertent use obsolete documents obsolete-but-still-in-use is the single most common non-compliance.

Document definition: In this sense, a "document" is an instruction of some sort (e.g., any information where an unauthorized change could cause a problem).

Example documents: Quality manual, procedures, project plans, national or International Standards (e.g. ISO 9001), industry specific codes-of-practice, customer specifications, drawings, software, examples of visual standards, among others..

I am not suggesting that you need to be ISO 9000 certified (you may and in some industries it is a requirement to be a supplier), but there are useful practices you can learn from.

Manual Document Control System

This system is a little out of date with the advent of internet and intranet, but it still works well. The apparent advantage is that there are no direct costs but when analyzed, it may be more expensive than the computerized model because of the time investment. With this system you have a series of three-ring binders easily accessible to all employees. When an SOP or Process Map is changed, someone must be responsible for placing the revisions in each manual.

Manual systems can be inefficient, requiring tremendous man-hours in terms of routing documents, obtaining approval and signatures, face-to-face meetings to discuss changes, and search and retrieval of documents during inspections and audits.

This might be the way you begin the process but in time, you will want to utilize a computerized version that automates the process.

Electronic Document Control System

There are countless advantages for utilizing a computerized Document Control System.

Electronic Document Control Software Systems automates routing, delivery, escalation, and approval of documents. It can handle all types of documents regardless of the software used to create them. Most systems feature a centralized, secure repository that allows search and retrieval easy during inspections and audits.

A good software system will provide automatic revision control to ensure that only the current version of a document is available. Changes can be initiated and approved electronically, and the system should track all changes and make them available through reports. You must ensure that all users are able to access the necessary document any time.

One advantage of internet based systems is that any employee with access to the internet can view, update, and approve documents. This is a great feature for management while traveling and for remote facilities.

There are some great systems available, and I encourage you to Google "document control systems" and you will find many systems to choose from. Find one that best fits your budget and needs.

Action Items

- ☑ *Create a list of your Key Processes*
- ☑ *Ask a team of employees to document your current procedures using an agreed upon template*
- ☑ *Create Process Maps of your key processes*

- ☑ *Create a Document Control System with a review process to keep SOPs and Process Maps current*

- ☑ *List actions you plan to take on your Action List Worksheet (or Action Planning tool you selected) and set the appropriate dates and steps you plan to take*

Chapter 9
Employee Base

In this chapter, I will discuss the role of your employees. As mentioned in an earlier chapter, anyone can purchase the same equipment and technology that you possess, and they can open up across the street and compete directly with you. However, there are two primary aspects that they do not possess: your employees and your customers. You must make sure that the potential buyer feels comfortable with your employee base.

Buyer's Perspective

- *The buyer will want to know that employees will stay when the owner leaves*
- *They will not want to have to deal with unproductive employees or discipline issues when they begin to manage the business*
- *The prospective buyer will want to inherit a legacy of satisfied and skilled employees*
- *They will want to know there is a training system in place to increase employee skill levels in this competitive environment*

As I mentioned in the chapter on developing leaders, Jim Collins book, *Good to Great* offers a great insight into how we should go about employee selection. In this book, Collins describes the analogy of the bus. The bus is your business and you must make sure:

- You have the right people on the bus

- They are in the right seats
- The wrong people need to be moved to another bus
- You must make sure the bus is going in the right direction

Should You Tell Your Employees?

Most of the business brokers I have talked with believe it is best not to share with employees that you are selling your business. There is a risk of losing key employees during the sale and could jeopardizing the entire transaction.

The Right Employees

Between now and the time you begin the process of selling your business, you must ensure that the employees you currently have and those you might hire are the right employees. The material for this section "The Right Employees" and "Testing" was provided courtesy of Norm Bobay, president of hireMAX.

The Talent Management Cycle

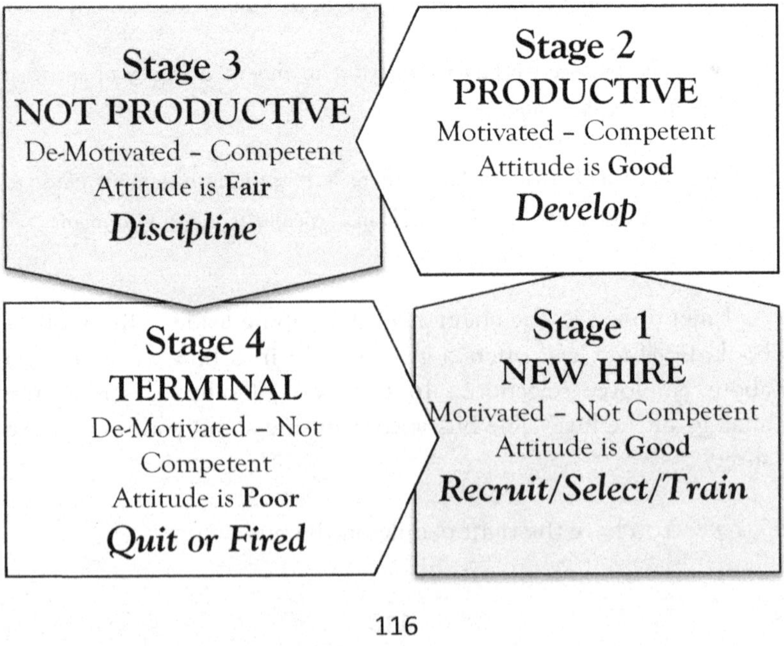

The above Employee Cycle illustrates the stages employees can go through during the time they are with your company. Stages Three and Four are draining and costly to an organization. Obviously, you want to move all your employees to the Stage Two and keep them there. That is determined by how well they are managed in Stage Two and selected for hire in Stage One.

Assignment - Create a list of all your employees and indicate which stage you feel they are in. Were you surprised? To verify your list, you might ask another manager to perform the same exercise and compare the results.

As a leader who is preparing your business to be at maximum value, you have to perform the following:

- Effectively move Stage One employees to Stage Two
- Keep Stage Two employees in that position
- Move Stage Three employees back to Stage Two
- Remove all employees in Stage Four (move to Stage Two if possible)

Stage 4 - Terminal

Employees in this stage damage your company; if you listed anyone that fits in this category, you need to take action immediately. They are poisoning your entire environment and making it difficult to motivate all your employees.

You need to accept that poor management may be responsible for letting employees arrive at this stage, but you must do something about it even if you helped create the situation.

These employees are likely to be unhappy and would jump ship (or bus) at the first opportunity. If there is no hope of moving them out of this stage, you must take the necessary steps to help them move on.

Why Employees Leave
In a study performed by Harvard Business Review, it was discovered that employees leave for the following reasons:

- 1% Die
- 3% Move away
- 5% Personal problems
- 9% Find a better job
- 14% One bad encounter
- 68% Management indifference, rudeness or lack of assistance

Stage Four is costly and you run the risk of a lawsuit if not handled properly. In order to avoid this stage, hire better in Stage One; manage effectively in Stage Two; and document employee warnings in Stage Three.

Stage 3 - Non Productive

Why Employees Become Dissatisfied

- Wrong job match
- Ill-equipped
- Mismanaged
- Personal reasons
- No established relationships

The cost of disengagement
Employee disengagement is costly. Current studies indicate that employees are disengaged an average of 10 hours per week, and their disengagement is demonstrated in the following ways:

- Long lunch breaks
- Lingering bathroom trips
- Unauthorized internet use (emails, Facebook, games, among others)
- Water cooler conversations
- Meaningless paper shuffling

The following are some conservative cost estimates:

$ 12.00 Per Hour
x's 10 Hours (Current estimation)
= **$120 Per Week**
= **$6240 Per Year Per Employee**

This does not even include the costs of benefits. Assess the costs for your employees:

Average employee hourly wage		________
Average hourly benefit costs	+	________
	Total	________
Disengaged hours per week	X	10
Per employee estimate	Total	________
Number of employees	X	________
Total estimate monthly cost		________
Projected annual cost	X 12	________

You must take this issue seriously and make an effort to reduce employee disengagement. Enhance management involvement in Stage Two and consider measuring attitudes towards work in Stage One.

Stage 2 - Productive
Motivated – Competent
Attitude - Good

In Harvard's research on the effectiveness of training, they found the following benefits for companies that effectively train their employees over their competitors:

- Growth rates **60-300%**
- Return on assets **150-300%**
- Return on sales **200-300%**
- Service, quality, customer satisfaction increased by **50%**

This 1990's quote from Ken Blanchard, author of the book "The One Minute Manager," is just as true today as it was then:

"If I had to give the single most important lesson for survival in the 90"s I would say. Try to focus on the difference an individual manager can make on others in his or her individual work environment, whether it is ***through catching people doing things right*** *or realizing that none of us is as smart as all of us."*

Appreciation is the **#1** aspect employees say they want most on employment surveys!

Stage 1 – New Hire

It is important that all new hires are the right fit for your company and the prospective buyer will be impressed with a strong hiring process.

"Like an archer who wounds at random is he who hires a fool or passer-by" Proverbs 26:10

New employees begin in this stage as:

- Motivated – but Not Competent (yet)
- Attitude - Good

Analyze the lifetime cost of any new employee and treat them as an investment, not how much you will pay them per hour. If you hire someone whose salary and benefits total $30,000 a year, they will have received $300,000 in 10 years. Think of every employee as a minimum of a quarter of a million dollar investment. Do not take it lightly. Many people have a tendency to hire quickly to fill a spot, but this practice can be devastating to the long-term success of your company.

To hire the right employees you must:

Pre-Plan - Define the Job before you hire!

Have clear Job descriptions with duties and expectations

- What skills are required?
- What experience is needed?
- What behaviors does this job require?

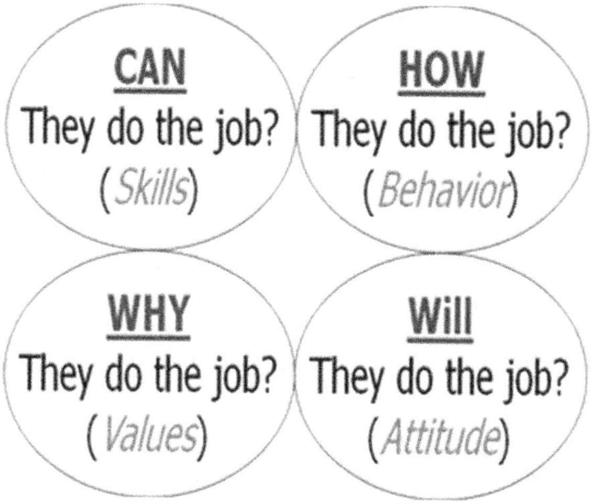

Testing - Match Candidates to the Job

To ensure you have the right match, you must perform a test applicable to the job requirements. You can test potential new hires and current employees to ensure their attitudes and skills match the job requirements.

Types of tests

Hard skills (intelligence)
Education – ***What*** we know about it
Experience – ***Where*** we have done it

Soft skills (personality)
Behavior – ***How*** we do it
Values – ***Why*** we do it
Attitude – ***Will*** we do it

Why use testing?

- Reduce turnover costs
- Candidate screening convenience
- Select good potential candidates
- Interview objectivity
- Individualized training

I want to illustrate what top of the line employee testing should entail. The following charts and graphs are from a leading provider of employee testing. This company provides the following:

- Feedback regarding work-related personality and intellectual abilities
- Competency-based reports provide additional insight into those factors that help or hinder the display of job-specific competencies
- Structured Interview Guides and Interview Probes to facilitate the interview process
- Management Suggestions to help with on-boarding new hires
- Additional Customization options: validate a success profile, develop custom norms

Personality & Skill Assessment Graph

- Optional intellectual ability assessment
- Measures 25+ characteristics which impact behavior
- Reports interpret these results in the context of the desired competencies
- Normed against a database of professionals/managers
- Available in 12 different languages
- Ongoing U.S. and international validation research

Intellectual Abilities

This type of testing is designed to integrate seven different ability tests, a feature that is unique to their system. Depending upon the requirements of the position and the time available for testing, a candidate may be given any combination of these tests.

- Critical Thinking
- Abstract Thinking
- Mental Alertness
- Verbal Comprehension
- Verbal Reasoning
- Arithmetic Reasoning
- Numerical Ability

Contact me and I will be glad to share samples of testing that is "best in class." I have developed a strategic alliance with the best in the industry.

Employee Satisfaction

I have discussed why employees leave and the high cost of disengagement; now, I want to discuss employee satisfaction. It has been my experience that the ideal approach is to measure employee satisfaction.

Just as I illustrated with customer satisfaction, you have the option of creating your own survey process or using a professional survey company. The advantages of hiring an outside firm are the following:

- Employees will feel safer more likely to answer honestly
- May offer comparisons with other companies (your industry or "World Class")
- Help in analyzing results

If you choose to create your own survey, the following will provide you with some ideas.

Employee Survey Questions

The first challenge is selecting the right set of questions to ask your employees. The purpose of the survey is to learn what areas they may possess some level of dissatisfaction in order for you to enact the necessary steps to improve in that area.

Below is a sample survey with some generic questions that you will want to start with and then develop further. Some may not be relevant to your industry and can be eliminated. This survey uses the Likert five point scale.

1 – Strongly Disagree
2 – Somewhat Disagree
3 – Neutral (either agree or disagree)
4 – Agree
5 – Strongly Agree

Question	1	2	3	4	5
I receive useful and constructive feedback from my manager.					
I am given adequate feedback about my performance.					
I receive feedback that helps me improve my					

performance.					
I have an opportunity to participate in the goal setting process.					
Employee performance evaluations are fair and appropriate.					
My supervisor gives me praise and recognition when I do a good job.					
When I do a good job, I receive the praise and recognition I deserve.					
Teamwork is encouraged and practiced in this organization.					
There is a strong feeling of teamwork and cooperation in this organization.					
People are held accountable for the quality of work they produce.					
The quality of our products and services are very important to this organization.					
In this organization we maintain very high standards of quality.					
This organization understands its customers' needs.					
This organization is extremely focused on its customers' needs.					
Customer needs are the top priority in this organization.					
I have a good understanding of the mission and the goals of this organization.					
I understand how my work directly contributes to the overall success of the organization.					
My job is important in accomplishing the mission of the organization.					
My supervisor provides me regular information about the mission and the goals of this organization.					
I am familiar with and understand the					

organization's strategic goals.					
Doing my job well gives me a sense of personal satisfaction.					
I am paid fairly for the work I do.					
My salary is competitive with similar jobs I might find elsewhere.					
I understand my benefit plan.					
I am satisfied with my benefit package.					
I have the resources I need to do my job well.					
The necessary information systems are in place and accessible for me to get my job done.					
I have all the information I need to do my job effectively.					
My workplace is well maintained.					
My workplace is a physically comfortable place to work.					
My workplace is safe.					
Information and knowledge are shared openly within this organization.					
Communication is encouraged in this organization.					
My manager does a good job of sharing information.					
Senior management communicates well with the rest of the organization.					
I have adequate opportunities for professional growth in this organization.					
I receive the training I need to do my job well.					
My manager is actively interested in my professional development and advancement.					
My manager encourages and supports my development.					
I am encouraged to learn from my mistakes					
My work is challenging.					

My work is stimulating.					
My work is rewarding.					
I have a mentor at work.					
The environment in this organization supports a balance between work and personal life.					
My manager understands the importance of maintaining a balance between work and personal life					
I am able to satisfy both my job and family responsibilities.					
I am not forced to choose between job and family obligations.					
The pace of the work in this organization enables me to do a good job					
The amount of work I am asked to do is reasonable					
The organization has reasonable expectations of its employees.					
My job does not cause unreasonable amounts of stress in my life.					
My manager treats all his/her employees fairly.					
The organization's policies for promotion and advancement are always fair.					
Favoritism (special treatment) is not an issue in raises or promotions.					
My manager is always consistent when administering policies concerning employees.					
I am always treated fairly by my manager.					
Everybody is treated fairly in this organization.					
I respect the senior leaders of this organization.					
I respect my manager as a competent professional.					
The leaders of this organization know what					

they are doing.					
Our senior managers demonstrate strong leadership skills					
I am very satisfied with my manager.					
My manager always treats me with respect.					
My manager listens to what I'm saying.					
This organization respects its employees.					
My manager values my talents and the contribution I make.					
My talent is valued at work.					
The organization values the contribution I make.					
My coworkers care about me as a person.					
People who challenge the status quo are valued.					
I can disagree with my supervisor without fear of getting in trouble.					
I am comfortable sharing my opinions at work.					
We work to attract, develop, and retain people with diverse backgrounds.					
People with different ideas are valued in this organization.					
My ideas and opinions count at work.					

You want to also include open-ended questions that provide additional and valuable information. You can design your own but below are a few suggestions:

- What is the most difficult challenge you face working here?
- What one aspect would you change if you could?
- What is the best aspect about working here?

Would you recommend this company to your family and friends? If not, why not?

Tabulating the Score

A great way to calculate your survey score is to compile the data into a spreadsheet with a column for each participating company and then average the scores. Convert the averages into a percentage by multiplying the average by 20.

Example:

Question	1	2	3	4	5	Ave	Score
My manager listens to what I'm saying.	4	3	3	5	3	3.6	72%
This organization respects its employees.	3	2	4	3	4	3.2	64%

Go to http://businessforsaleblueprint.com/book-resources for a spreadsheet that will calculate this for you.

Employee Focus Group

To obtain the most out of your survey you need to bring in a third party to conduct an employee focus group. This can sometimes be performed by Human Resources but you may still deal with employees feeling uncomfortable sharing their feelings and experiences.

Analyze the survey with the employee and discuss where they scored low and ask them to clarify and take notes. For example: Why do you feel the company only scored a 64% on employees feeling that the organization respects them? You will leave with useful ideas on how to improve your satisfaction level and an improved relationship with your employees. Compile the notes with no names of participants and have the management team review the results.

Tips

- Create action plans for the areas that need immediate improvement.
- When you make changes or improvements because of the survey, make sure to communicate that to employees, and they will be even more involved in the process next time.
- Make it an annual process

This is another great tool to show a prospective buyer because it demonstrates that:

- You take your employees satisfaction seriously
- You take action on areas that need improvement
- They notice areas where you excel

Performance Review System

Another important item to have established for your employees is a systematic approach to evaluating and reviewing employee performance.

The following are my recommendations for creating a good performance review system.

- Start with professional advice
- You establish the goal of the system (improve communication, performance, moral)
- Benchmark effective systems in yours or other industries
- Keep it simple and easy to understand
- Don't let it get overly paper intensive
- Keep the language easy to understand
- Make sure it is fair and meets legal requirements
- Has data driven decision making
- Reviewed to ensure it meets stated goals
- Holds employees accountable for performance
- Links performance results to companywide goals (where possible)

- Good document control

There is a plethora of useful information on the web and many good books on the subject. You may also want to contact a HR professional for additional help. The objective is to start your documented performance review system, and allow the benefits of it to hit long before you place your business on the market.

Employee Training Plans

I will not analyze in detail the issue of training but I must discuss the need for training. The Harvard study I mentioned earlier bears repeating. Their research found a strong correlation between employee training and the following:

- Growth rates **60-300%**
- Return on assets **150-300%**
- Return on sales **200-300%**
- Service, quality, customer satisfaction increased by **50%**

This matches the correlation I have also observed with Malcolm Baldrige National Quality Award winning organizations.

There are many practical resources for employee training. Review the training methods and resources discussed in Chapter #4.

Employee Skills Matrix

I recommend creating a Skills Matrix for each of your employees. It is simple, but highly effective tool to assess training needs, and it is easily reviewed, updated, and it presents the skills of team members in a single chart.

A Skills Matrix is a table that clearly shows the skills held by individuals in a team, and the skills gaps within a team.

A Skills Matrix will help you to:

- Review the skills and competences required for roles within the team
- Assess training needs
- Identify gaps in skills within the team
- Build commitment to the development of new skills.

Key steps in preparing a Skills Matrix

To get the most out of your Skills Matrix you will need to:

- Identify the job roles in your team
- Review and code standards of performance
- Assess the requirement for on-the-job training.

The following is a sample of how symbols are used to visually show skill levels:

Level	Description	Criteria	Symbol
0	Cannot Do	Insufficient knowledge or experience to perform to standard	○
1	Knows all elements of task	Has fully reviewed instructions, and is familiar with tools of the job	◔
2	Can to the basics	Has received instruction from a level 4 instructor	◑
3	Can do fully	Qualified by a lever 4 instructor to do task without supervision	◕

4	Can teach others ho to do	Has been approved by management to teach others	●

This is a great tool and can be used to get a visual on employee skill levels. Many manufacturing environments will post a matrix like this outside a work station or in a department. It will list the employee's names on the left and key skills necessary across the top. The rating similar to what is shown above will be listed for each skill. This makes it very easy to see if an employee is performing a task they have not yet qualified.

As mentioned before, many resources are available to help you with this.

Action Items

- ❑ *Evaluate the stage your current employees are in*
- ❑ *Take action to move all employees to Stage Two*
- ❑ *Remove employees that are stuck in Stage Four*
- ❑ *Consider utilizing a testing process for new hires to insure they are the right fit*
- ❑ *Review or develop a Performance Review System*
- ❑ *Evaluate your training program and create a Skills Matrix for each employee*
- ❑ *List actions you plan to take on your Action List Worksheet (or Action Planning tool you selected) and set the appropriate dates and steps you plan to take*

Chapter 10

Supplier Relationships

In this chapter, I will discuss your suppliers and the important part they play in the value of your business.

Buyer's Perspective

- *The buyer needs to know that critical supplier relationships will continue after the purchase of the business*
- *They need to evaluate the risks to the company if a supplier:*
  - *Went out of business*
  - *Dramatically raised prices*
  - *Significantly increased lead times*
- *The buyer will also want to evaluate strategic partners and how they would affect the business if that relationship changed*

The best way to discuss and analyze the importance of your supplier relationships to the value of your business is learn from a valuation expert. I asked Jeffrey H. Harwell, AVA (Accredited Valuation Analyst), managing Principle of Harwell & Company, to describe how he analyzes suppliers in determining the value of a business. The following is Harwell's answer:

"Without getting too complicated, the supplier issue in valuation typically impacts the determination of the discount rate applicable to the earnings stream. The lower the discount/capitalization rate the higher the estimated value of the enterprise. Now the question becomes how a supplier relationship could increase the discount rate?

- *Single captive supplier (similar to single or captive customer)*
- *Key supplier (supplier who represents a relatively large percentage of the enterprise's source of raw materials or products)*
- *Offshore supplier (logistic and other identifiable risks related to international location)*
- *Unionized supplier*

How a supplier relationship risk might be offset.

- *Diversify product line to diversify supplier source risk*
- *Diversify suppliers and relationships by number and location (assuming no logistical cost differences)*
- *Domestic supplier backup for the offshore supplier*
- *Non-unionized supplier*
- *JIT/Supply Chain/Lean production and operating process evaluation of suppliers*
- *Annual to bi-annual RFQ (Request for Quote) from suppliers (keep them honest)*
- *Annual or quarterly purchase order system for scheduled releases (monthly, weekly, etc)*

The supplier risk factor is one of approximately ten items that might increase the discount rate under the valuator's Company Specific Risk Premium (CSRP) which is a subjective area of the valuation. The supplier risk will typically be neutral or be increased by 1%-2%, if the valuator believes that the risk is greater than would be present in a publicly traded or professionally run enterprise. There lies the answer to your question from a valuation perspective. Reduce or eliminate the risk and reduce any points added to the discount rate related to supplier risk.

Also, the price being charged by suppliers impacts the margin of the enterprise which in turn is another one of the CSRP elements. If the enterprise is a franchise, there is a chance the supplier may be exclusive which could impact both the balance sheet and income statement from a valuation perspective".

Supplier Relationship Management

SRM (Supplier Relationship Management) is a systematic approach to managing an enterprise's interactions with the organizations that supply the goods and services to your company. The goal of (SRM) is to improve processes between your company and your suppliers.

SRM includes the information flow of supply chain management (SCM). A good SRM system helps to increase the efficiency of processes associated with purchasing supplies, materials and services, managing inventory, and processing materials.

An effective SRM system can have a customer satisfaction impact, especially when it reduces costs, improves quality, and/or delivery times.

I recommend you do some research on how SRM could help your company. The larger your supplier interactions, the greater the potential benefit to your company.

Supplier Approval Process

Most companies do not possess a formal Supplier Approval Process. While this process is more common in larger companies with purchasing department, some sort of disciplined process will provide you with a great deal of value.

Many companies will buy from anyone that has the lowest price without a detailed analysis of their quality and reputation.

Critical Suppliers

I do not make a distinction from whom you buy your rubber bands and pens from, but I do make a distinction for suppliers whose products or services are critical to quality and customer satisfaction. These are the suppliers who need a little more scrutiny before making a purchase from them.

The following are some key questions you must ask yourself about critical suppliers:

- Will this supplier make us look good to our customers?
- Will they deliver on time as promised?
- Will their quality meet or exceed customer requirements?

I have seen many customer relationships ruined by a poor supplier or sub-contractor. To the customer, the supplier reflects on you. You cannot blame problems on the supplier, in the end, they are buying from you.

Let's explore a couple of examples:

- Your delivery service frequently delivers your products damaged
- One component part of your assembly has a high failure rate; the client sees the unit as a whole and you are the responsible party
- Your supplier goes from filling orders in three days to three weeks and you cannot deliver as promised
- Your contracted service arrives at the clients site, dirty, smelly, and ill tempered

For purchases that are critical to quality and customer satisfaction, I recommend you follow a formal Supplier Approval Process. This starts with creating Supplier Selection Criteria. The following are my recommendations for creating your selection criteria:

- Create a team of employees from different departments to create your companies criteria
- Find samples of criteria used by other organizations you benchmark with or resources you have found
- The team submits a draft of their recommendations
- Team creates a process map of the entire Supplier Selection Process

The following is commonly used supplier selection criteria:

- What is the past experience and performance with your needed product or service?
- A description of their quality system, including meeting regulatory requirements or mandated quality system registration (for example, ISO 9001, QS-9000)
- What is their ability to meet current and potential capacity requirements, and do so on the desired delivery schedule?
- Financial stability (this could be critical in certain circumstances)
- Total cost of dealing with the supplier (including material cost, communications methods, inventory requirements and incoming verification required).
- Does the supplier have a performance improvement process?
- Do they have a process for responding to Supplier Corrective Action Requests (SCAR)?

Things you might do in determining if the potential supplier fits your criteria:

- Ask for references of other customers served by the supplier
- Obtaining a Dun & Bradstreet or other publicly available financial report
- Requesting a formal quote, which includes providing the supplier with specifications and other requirements (for example, testing)
- Visits to the supplier by management and/or the selection team
- Confirmation of quality system status either by on-site assessment, a written survey or request for a certificate of quality system registration

The following is another great example of how you can find valuable examples on the internet.

A great example of a "World Class" Supplier Approval and Selection Process is found on the FedEx web site at:
http://www.fedex.com/us/supplier/selection.html

"FedEx Supplier Selection Process

FedEx is committed to reducing total costs through supply chain management excellence. FedEx defines supply chain management as managing the business process from the initial supplier to the ultimate customer focusing on speed and flexibility, resulting in the lowest total cost and highest customer satisfaction-from supplier's supplier to customer's customer-with supply decisions based on total life cycle costs. FedEx identifies five principal attributes of supply chain management:

Strategy - *Creating an effective supply chain management organization and supporting fact-based strategies and plans.*

Resources - *Developing and deploying human resources and information systems necessary to maximize performance. Nothing happens without top-notch, highly-skilled professionals using effective technical tools.*

Processes - *Creating strategic plans based upon total cost management and insourcing/outsourcing analysis and applying a systematic approach to better utilizing the supply base.*

Optimization - *Aligning the supply base with our supply chain goals and continually seeking to improve the supply chain methods and composition.*

Globalization - *Viewing supply opportunities on a global basis.*

High standards for service and quality from FedEx suppliers will never be compromised. We at FedEx look for quality products and services delivered on time and at competitive prices resulting in the lowest total cost of ownership. FedEx selects its suppliers based on their ability to meet our stringent requirements and the capability to serve as a supply chain improvement partner.

Before contacting FedEx about being a supplier, you should ask yourself:

- *'Do I have a product or service that FedEx needs?'*
- *'Do I have the resources to supply these needs in sufficient quantities as well as the support service required?'*
- *'Can I truly bring sufficient value to FedEx to reduce its total cost of ownership?'"*

Create your own supplier questionnaire; the following are some sample questions that may or may not apply to your industry.

- Basic company information of course
- Contact information
- Company headquarters
- Type of ownership?
- Number of employees?
- Annual gross sales revenue?
- Total amount of product liability insurance? Insurance applied to what country(ies)?
- What internationally recognized quality and/or environment certification awarded?
- Describe the capabilities or you organization:
- List 2 to 4 customer references:
- Company status? (M/W/V= Minority, Woman, or Service Veteran owned business)
- Percentage total purchases last fiscal year form M/W/V?
- Number of shifts at this facility
- Do you use and information system for manufacturing control?
- Dou you sub-contract any part of your business?
- Manufacturing lead time (from order receipt to product available for shipping)?
- Do you have a high speed internet connection?

- List production activity interruptions (vacation, holiday, and scheduled plant shut downs)?
- Do you manage customer inventories?
- Do you have a quality system?
- Do you have a training plan (including for temporaries) to fit needed skills?
- Do you review your capability to meet the customer's requirements before accepting a contract or order?
- Are changes n the customer's requirements recorded and confirmations transmitted back to the customer?
- Do you have clearly defined quality acceptance criteria?
- Do you have critical to quality processes and procedures documented?
- Are design changes documented and controlled?
- Do you have a receiving process that insures parts and materials meet specified requirements?
- Are final inspections and test performed before shipment?
- Are internal non-conformities indentified, treated and controlled (including repairs and rejects)?
- Do you have a corrective and preventive action process?
- To you ask your suppliers for corrective actions when you receive non-conforming product?
- Have you identified the significant environmental aspects or your activity (emission to air, emissions to water, waste, noise, etc.) and are your waste and effluents treated or eliminated in compliance with the regulation?
- Can you estimate the following flows for each product: recycled material content, manufacturing power, water consumption, special waste quantity, ordinary waste quantity and recyclability?
- Are you capable of providing the detailed composition of your products?
- Do you have a security system?

As you can see, there are many questions you can ask a supplier. Form a brainstorming team to discuss these and other questions that are appropriate for your suppliers.

Supplier Value Relationship

At the beginning of this chapter I quote Jeff Harwell on how the supplier relationship can impact the valuation of your business, the following is his thoughts on things you might do:

"How a supplier relationship risk might be offset.

- ☑ Diversify product line to diversify supplier source risk
- ☑ Diversify suppliers and relationships by number and location (assuming no logistical cost differences)
- ☑ Domestic supplier backup for the offshore supplier
- ☑ Non-unionized supplier
- ☑ JIT/Supply Chain/Lean production and operating process evaluation of suppliers
- ☑ Annual to bi-annual RFQ (Request for Quote) from suppliers (keep them honest)
- ☑ Annual or quarterly purchase order system for scheduled releases (monthly, weekly, etc)"

Jeff has provided you with the formula on how to keep away from a supplier related discount rate. Arrange your management team and purchasing supervisor (if applicable) to review the above items and discuss how you might offset some risks by either your selection process or some internal processes you may implement.

SCAR (Supplier Corrective Action Request)

An important element in your Supplier System is to have a formal supplier request for corrective action when a product or service is non-conforming.

When a supplier fails to meet your requirements in quality or service, you should issue them a corrective action request that must be completed by a specific time and include a full analysis of the failure noted on the request. Once the analysis is completed the corrective action document must be sent to you by the due date listed on the SCAR.

A complete SCAR includes the following information:

Short Term/Containment Action
A short term/containment action is an action that immediately prevents the customer from receiving any more non-conforming product.

Examples of Containment:

- Quarantine and sort inventories
- Implement 100% inspection
- Address in-transit material

Root Cause Analysis
Ask your supplier to perform a Root Cause Analysis (RCA) in the process of discovery. What happened, why did it happen, and how can it be prevented using the basic premise that errors and failures that occur are a result of the process, not simply the action or the people. It is best to analyze a defined problem with different people to obtain different perspectives. More times than not, problems have more than one root cause. Fixing multiple root causes provide greater assurance the problem will not reoccur.

Root Cause Analysis is a three-step process:

1. Define the problem (What?)
2. Ask Questions (Three Legged Five Why)
3. Corrective and Preventative Action (How? - Answer each leg of the Five Why form)

Problem definition is the basis of all effective corrective actions. Without a clearly defined problem, it is difficult or nearly impossible to develop an effective corrective action.

The key to discovering the root cause is asking "Why" enough times that the permanent corrective action to fix the problem becomes obvious. The general rule is three to five times or more.

Examples of tools to help reach a root cause are:

- Fishbone Diagram
- Cause and Effect Table
- SIPOC Chart* (Supplier, Input, Process, Output, Customer)

What constitutes a "good" corrective action?

- Containment Action is taken right away
- Corrective Action addresses the identified Root Cause
- Involves a permanent change in the process
- Prevents the problem reoccurrence on the product and similar products
- Is implemented prior to the SCAR being closed

Contact me and I would be glad to share a sample SCAR form with you or a quick web search will provide you with many great examples.

Action Items

☑ *Review your current process for selecting suppliers*

☑ *Create and document you own Supplier Approval/Selection Process*

☑ *Create a Supplier Approval Questionnaire*

☑ *Review how you might offset Supplier Risks in your selection and purchasing processes*

☑ *Develop a SCAR form for supplier non-conforming products or services*

☑ *List actions you plan to take on your Action List Worksheet (or Action Planning tool you selected) and set the appropriate dates and steps you plan to take*

Chapter 11
Equipment & Technology

In this chapter, I will discuss the importance of maintaining your equipment and technology needs. Many business owners are reluctant to maintain and care for their equipment in order to preserve cash. I realize there is a balancing act to deal with but one that needs careful analysis.

Buyer's Perspective

- *The buyer needs to know that there will not be major expenses on equipment and technology after the purchase of the company*
- *They want to know the equipment is well maintained*
- *It is important to know that software is not only current but is properly licensed*
- *They want to be assured that the equipment and technology is current and/or exceeds that of your competition*

Equipment Evaluation

At some point in the sale process an expert equipment appraiser may be called in to evaluate your equipment. Now is the time for you and your team complete a self- evaluation of all your key equipment. You can utilize your own criteria of what you consider key, but for now, analyze anything that would cost more than $2,000 to replace.

The following are aspects you will need to evaluate:

- Grade the mechanical condition of the equipment.

A = Excellent
B= Good
C = Fair
D = Poor
F = Must Replace

- Estimate the useful life of equipment in years

- Grade the overall appearance of the equipment
  A = Excellent
  B= Good
  C = Fair
  D = Poor
  F = Very Poor

- Rate what you and your team feel should be done with the equipment prior to placing the business on the market
  Replace
  Repair
  Clean/Paint
  Nothing

- Estimate cost of actions needed

- Create action plans and assignments for the items you determined need to be addressed

- Prioritize repairs and replacement based on cash flow and immediate needs

Include the information in a form similar to the sample below and use it to execute next step decisions.

Equipment Name	Cond	Life	Looks	Cost	Priority
IT server	A	2 yrs	A	$16,000	Low
Fork lift	C	7	D	$2,500	Med
Parts Press	D	5	D	$123,000	High

Preventive Maintenance Program (PM)

It is important to demonstrate to the prospective buyer that you have a systematic approach toward the maintenance of equipment. Preventive maintenance will help reduce equipment downtime and unscheduled maintenance. You will need to create a maintenance program that is documented and followed (accountability is required).

Preventive maintenance is a schedule of planned maintenance actions aimed at the prevention of breakdowns and failures. The primary goal of preventive maintenance is to prevent the failure of equipment before it occurs. It is designed to preserve and enhance equipment reliability by the replacement of worn components before they fail. PM activities include equipment checks, partial or complete overhauls at specified periods, oil changes, lubrication, among others. In addition, workers can record equipment deterioration in order to replace or repair worn parts before they cause system failure. Recent technological advances in tools for inspection and diagnosis have enabled even more accurate and effective equipment maintenance. The ideal preventive maintenance program would prevent all equipment failure before it occurs.

Value of Preventive Maintenance

There are multiple misconceptions about preventive maintenance. One such misconception is that PM is unduly costly. This logic dictates that it would cost more for regularly scheduled downtime and maintenance than it would normally cost to operate equipment until repair is absolutely necessary. This may be true for some components; however, one should compare not only the costs but the long-term benefits and savings associated with preventive maintenance. Without preventive maintenance, for example, costs for lost production time from unscheduled equipment breakdown will be incurred. Also, preventive maintenance will result in savings due to an increase of effective system service life.

Long-term benefits of preventive maintenance include:

- Improved system reliability
- Decreased cost of replacement
- Decreased system downtime
- Better spares inventory management

Long-term effects and cost comparisons usually favor preventive maintenance over performing maintenance actions only when the system fails.

A simple log for each piece of equipment along with a document that describes what action is necessary and during what time intervals may impact the success of your business. To ensure this is sustained, you should ask someone to audit this process every couple of months.

Equipment Maintenance Log

Equipment Description:______________________________

Serial #:______________________Model #:______________

Date:	Action Taken/Comments:	Initials

Total Productive Maintenance (TPM)

If you possess expensive equipment where downtime is costly (money and effect on meeting customer schedules), you may need to proceed to the next step 'in preventive maintenance, which is Total Productive Maintenance (TPM).

The primary goal of TPM is to prevent unplanned downtime. I have seen situations where right in the middle of a giant production project, a machine goes down and simple part has to be flown in from overseas. What would happen in your company if a critical piece of equipment went down for a day or a week? If the answer to that question is "it would be devastating", then you should investigate TPM. Find a TPM consultant in your area. One source would be to check with your local MEP (Manufacturing Extension Partnership) for help in this area.

Technology Assessment

Technology is often analyzed from the IT (Information Technology) perspective but it can also relate to the technology used in equipment. Assess the technology used in your business and ask yourself the following questions:

- Is our technology current with our competitors?
- Does our technology provide any type of competitive advantage?
- What technology is on the horizon that could dramatically alter our industry?
- What items are on our wish list for future enhancements of software or equipment?
- Is our IT security system sufficient?
- Does our data backup process sufficiently protect in cases of fire, theft or damage?
- Does the electrical system have sufficient protection from power surges and outages?

- Is our system capable of handling increased growth?

Professional IT Assessment

There are many companies that will perform free or low cost assessment of your current IT infrastructure. This would be an important area to obtain an outside perspective. Of course, their objective is to sell you some software or equipment but that is up to you to determine if it is necessary and financially feasible.

I asked my friend Steve Moreau (Director of Technology at Networking Results, Inc.) to share his thoughts on assessing technology, and the following is his perspective:

"When assessing your technology be methodical and objective. Focus on two key areas 1) Exposure and 2) Value.

Exposure includes the method of securing company data, licensing compliance, acceptable use policies and method of enforcement, single points of failure, threat prevention and mitigation. Any one of these areas has the potential to expose the business owner/manager to law suit, loss of employee productivity, and/or theft of business critical or confidential data. What the assessment may reveal is there may be deficiencies in more than one of the areas, compounding the exposure to your business. Assessing your exposure is more tactical in nature, and may reveal things that need to be prioritized and addressed quickly. If exposure is more tactical, value is more strategic.

Assessing value of technology is more art than science. The value of technology is how well your tools are supporting your business versus the cost of the technology. Cost of technology includes the initial cost of the solution and any ongoing maintenance and support required to keep it running. Like buying a car, technology investment does not stop with the initial purchase. This is why the assessment of technology value is so important. More than just a return on investment (ROI) study, this goes to the very heart of the efficiency of your business operations. If you have ever thought, "There has got to be an easier or better way to do this", there usually always is. Technology is mature enough that we are not developing many new solutions that will radically change your business. There are advancements in solutions that are beneficial and useful, but are more analogous to the turning of a dial for adjustment versus the changing an entire business process like the initial introduction of a new technology solution may do.

The question that needs to be asked and answered is, "Are my technology tools effective in helping the company achieve the most important goals and objectives"? The answer will be yes, no, or maybe. Yes is great news. No is going to be expensive. Maybe is more often the answer and really means that you are doing some things right, but adjustments in technology or use of that technology may yield better results.

The topic of Open Source (some free, some not) solutions invariably comes up in the assessment of technology value. There are many Open Source solutions that are viable solutions to run a business on today, however the initial savings in licensing costs do not paint the entire picture. The astute business owner/manager must also factor in the cost of maintenance, administration, support, and effectiveness of the solution in the assessment of value. In short, when assessing technology, approach it as any other business tool. That is the key to having technology be a true business asset rather than an unknown "black hole" that seems to grow year-by-year."

In summary, look closely at all your equipment and technology and evaluate what actions may need to be taken prior to selling your business.

Action Items

- ❑ *Complete your own evaluation of equipment*
- ❑ *Establish a formal Equipment Maintenance Program, possibly including TPM*

Chapter 12
Additional Value Factors

In the previous chapters, I covered what I consider to be the most common value drivers to assess and improve in a business. Depending on your industry and the size of the company, there could be other factors to explore. These are also aspects a professional business valuation provider will analyze when he or she performs a business valuation.

Buyer's Perspective

Overall, the buyer is vigilant of every potential risk that may confront them in the future

The following are a few more factors that may move you toward a premium price for your business or cause it to be heavily discounted in value.

- Inventory
- Product mix
- Market conditions
- Proprietary processes, products or patents
- Industry Trends
- Warranties
- Facilities

Inventory

The buyer wants to confirm that inventory values are accurately portrayed

Depending on your type of business, inventory may or may not be an issue. A service company may have $2,500 in office supplies, while a manufacturing operation might have $2.5 million worth of parts in the warehouse.

Assess your inventory and clear out old and obsolete items that are of little or no value. If there is some value in keeping (it may be used someday), then make sure the value is correctly stated and not illustrated at the original purchase price

Product Mix and Innovation

This is another area that will vary greatly depending on your industry or service. Some businesses rely heavily on R&D (Research and Development) to create and introduce new products to the market, such as in the pharmaceutical and electronic areas. Both industries require new products to be released on a regular basis.

The buyer wants to confirm your products and services will not quickly become obsolete. They will pay a premium for a company that can demonstrate industry leadership in products and innovation

You can demonstrate innovation in any industry. The following is a description of Managing for Innovation, which is one of the core values of the Malcolm Baldrige National Quality Award for Performance Excellence:

"Managing for Innovation

Innovation means making meaningful change to improve an organization's products, services, programs, processes, and operations and to create new value for the organization's stakeholders. Innovation should lead your organization to new dimensions of performance. Innovation is no longer strictly the purview of research and development departments; innovation is important for all aspects of your operations and all work systems and work processes. Organizations should be led and managed so that innovation becomes part of the learning culture. Innovation should be integrated into daily work and should be supported by your performance improvement system.

Innovation builds on the accumulated knowledge of your organization and its people. Therefore, the ability to rapidly disseminate and capitalize on this knowledge is critical to driving organizational innovation"

Review your products and document areas in which your company has been innovative. If you have not been innovative, then begin to explore ways to incorporate innovation in your products or service

Market Conditions

Selling your business is all about timing. Selecting the best time to place your business on the market is key. Some business owners, who have a desperate need to sell their business right away for reasons such as medical or family issues, may not be able to select the best time. You will have the best chance to obtain a premium for your business if you can time the sale when the market is at a peak.

The chart below illustrates the importance of timing and how frequently EBITDA multiple averages change. I removed the multiplier amounts because these are much larger than my average reader can expect. The point I want you to see is that, on average 2001 and 2002 would not have been good years to receive a premium price for your business. If the option is available to you, try to time your sale when the market multiplier is the most favorable.

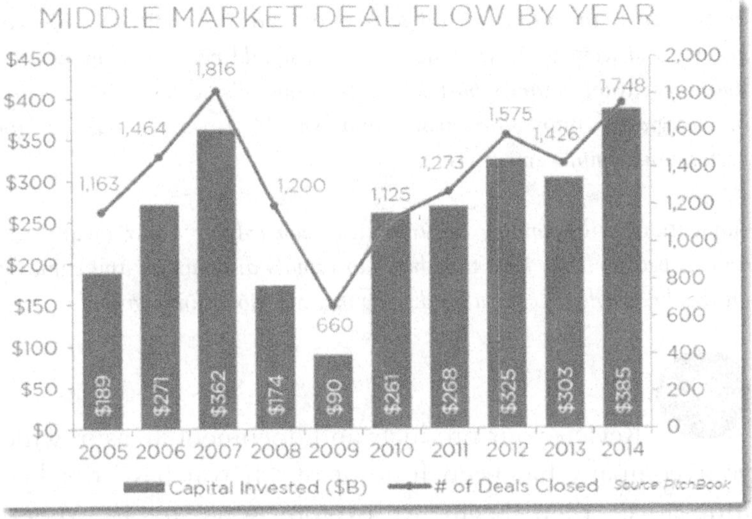

Source: PitchBook is an industry leading M&A research firm that focuses solely on private equity and related industry niches

Times of recession and/or tight capital are not the most effective times to place your business on the market. You would not have wanted to be trying to sell your business in 2008 and 2009.

Proprietary Processes, Products or Patents

Do you have a competitive advantage because of products or processes that you have patented and have exclusive rights you use?

The buyer will assess how products and services will stay competitive in the future.

Design a list of all your patents you own and their expatriation dates. Evaluate any possible products or processes you should file for patents

Industry Trends

While this is an item you have very little control of, I would like to make you aware of its possible impact on the value of your business. Are you in an industry that is growing or declining? An example of a declining industry would be the Newspaper business that has been declining for many years. Because of the aging population, the health care industry is expected to grow for many years. Become aware of how your industry is doing and understand the will impact values.

If possible, demonstrate how you countered industry trends or how you can capture market share and be profitable despite the industry.

You may be in a position to demonstrate that while your overall industry may be declining, your segment has great potential for growth and profit. For example, the printing industry as a whole is declining every year, but the short-run digital segment has been growing rapidly.

Warranties

Does your business have products or service warranties that will transfer to the buyer?

The buyer needs to be assured there are not large potential liabilities or even litigation on the horizon that need to be taken into consideration.

Assess outstanding warranties and the potential risk to the buyer. Document past warranty costs and actions you have taken that will reduce those costs in the future.

Conclusion

I hope you have found your time reading *Business For Sale Blueprint* to be a value to you. If you are the kind of person that is determined to get the highest possible value from your business, then I know your application of these strategies and ideas will yield tremendous results. It has been my great pleasure to provide information, tools and resources that I know will help you increase the value, stability and salability of your business.

I realize that statistics show many business owners will put this book on the shelf and follow very few of these recommendations. What excites me is to know that there is a percentage or readers who will apply the tools that best fit their situation, and:

- Sell their business that would not have otherwise
- Gain hundreds of thousands, even millions of dollars extra in the sale of their business
- Run their business more profitably with less stress

Every business has many opportunities for improvement. As I suggested at the beginning of this book, try not to let yourself feel overwhelmed. If you followed my suggestion to create an Action Plan, it is probably full of things you realize need to be done in your business. Prioritize, delegate, and methodically take them on one by one. Each accomplishment will make your business more valuable to you and a prospective buyer.

Please visit my website http://businessforsaleblueprint.com/book-resources for more information. I will continue to provide my readers and clients with information on how to improve the value of their business.

As mentioned several times throughout this book, be sure to take advantage of the resources I have made available only to *Business For Sale Blueprint* readers.

Please let me know how this book has impacted you and your business. I look forward to hearing your success story. Please feel free to contact me for any additional information, tools or service I can provide.

Fred Herbert
(817) 915-5123
fred@fredherbert.com
http://fredherbert.com
http://businessforsaleblueprint.com

Made in the USA
Monee, IL
04 November 2026

67380160R00095